Geographical Worlds

The Shape of the World Course Team

The Open University

John Allen	Senior Lecturer in Economic Geography and Course Team Chair
James Anderson	Senior Lecturer in Geography
Robin Arkle	Graphic Designer, BBC
Melanie Bayley	Editor
Brian Beeley	Senior Lecturer in Geography
Pam Berry	Compositor, TPS
Gail Block	Assistant Producer, BBC
John Blunden	Reader in Geography
Chris Brook	Lecturer in Geography
Margaret Charters	Course Secretary
Allan Cochrane	Senior Lecturer in Urban Studies
Debbie Crouch	Graphic Designer
Stuart Hall	Professor of Sociology
Chris Hamnett	Professor of Urban Geography
Fiona Harris	Editor
Christina Janoszka	Course Manager
Pat Jess	Lecturer in Geography
Jack Leathem	Producer, BBC
Michéle Marsh	Secretary
Doreen Massey	Professor of Geography
Anthony McGrew	Senior Lecturer in Politics
Diane Mole	Graphic Designer
Eleanor Morris	Series Producer, BBC
Ray Munns	Graphic Artist
Judith Rolph	Series Production Assistant, BBC
Philip Sarre	Senior Lecturer in Geography
Paul Smith	Media Librarian
Doreen Warwick	Discipline Secretary
Kathy Wilson	Production Assistant, BBC
Chris Wooldridge	Editor

External Assessor

Nigel Thrift	Professor of Geography, University of Bristol

Consultants

Rick Ball	Tutor Panel
Erlet Cater	Lecturer in Geography, University of Reading
Ray Hall	Senior Lecturer in Geography, University of London
Russell King	Professor of Geography, University of Sussex
Andrew Leyshon	Lecturer in Geography, University of Hull
Matthew Lockwood	Lecturer in Sociology, University of Sussex
Jenny Meegan	Tutor Panel
Richard Meegan	Senior Lecturer in Geography, University of Liverpool
Phil Pinch	Tutor Panel
Gillian Rose	Lecturer in Geography, University of Edinburgh
Steven Yearley	Professor of Sociology, University of Ulster

The Shape of the World: Explorations in Human Geography

Volume 1: Geographical Worlds

Edited by John Allen and Doreen Massey

Volume 2: A Shrinking World? Global Unevenness and Inequality

Edited by John Allen and Chris Hamnett

Volume 3: An Overcrowded World? Population, Resources and the Environment

Edited by Philip Sarre and John Blunden

Volume 4: A Place in the World? Places, Culture and Globalization

Edited by Doreen Massey and Pat Jess

Volume 5: A Global World? Re-ordering Political Space

Edited by James Anderson, Chris Brook and Allan Cochrane

Geographical Worlds

edited by
John Allen and Doreen Massey

The Open University OXFORD

The five volumes of the series form part of the second-level Open University course D215 *The Shape of the World*. If you wish to study this or any other Open University course, details can be obtained from the Central Enquiry Service, PO Box 200, The Open University, Milton Keynes, MK7 6YZ.

For availability of the video- and audiocassette materials, contact Open University Educational Enterprises Ltd (OUEE), 12 Cofferidge Close, Stony Stratford, Milton Keynes, MK11 1BY.

Oxford University Press, Walton Street, Oxford OX2 6DP

Oxford   New York

Athens   Auckland   Bangkok   Bombay
Calcutta   Cape Town   Dar es Salaam   Delhi
Florence   Hong Kong   Istanbul   Karachi
Kuala Lumpur   Madras   Madrid   Melbourne
Mexico City   Nairobi   Paris   Singapore
Taipei   Tokyo   Toronto
and associated companies in
Berlin   Ibadan

Oxford is a trade mark of Oxford University Press

Published in the United States
by Oxford University Press Inc., New York

Published in association with The Open University

First published 1995

Edited, designed and typeset by The Open University

Printed and bound in Great Britain by
The Bath Press, Avon

A catalogue record for this book is available from the British Library

Library of Congress Cataloguing in Publication Data applied for

ISBN 0 19 874185 5 (paper)

ISBN 0 19 874184 7 (cloth)

Geographical Worlds

Contents

Preface

Geographical Worlds is the first of five volumes in a new series of human geography teaching texts. The series, entitled *The Shape of the World: Explorations in Human Geography* is designed as an introduction to the principal themes of geographical thought: namely, those of space, place and the environment. The five volumes form the central part of an Open University course, with the same title as that of the series. Each volume, however, is free-standing and can be studied on its own or as part of a wide range of social science courses in universities and colleges.

The series is built around an exploration of many of the key issues which are shaping our world as we move into the twenty-first century and which, above all else, are geographical in character. Each volume in various ways engages with taken-for-granted notions such as those of nature, distance, movement, sustainability, the identity of places and local cultures to put together what may be referred to as the building blocks of our geographical imagination.

In fact, our understanding of the nature of the geographical imagination is one of three shared features which distinguish the five volumes as a series. In developing the contribution that geography can make to our understanding of a changing world and our place within it, each volume has something distinct to offer. A second feature of the volumes is that the majority of chapters include a number of selected readings – extracts drawn from books and articles – which relate closely to the line of argument and which are integral to the discussion as it develops. The relevant readings can be found at the end of the chapter to which they relate and are printed in two columns to distinguish them from the main teaching text. The third shared feature of the volumes is the student-orientated nature of the teaching materials. Each volume is intended as part of an interactive form of study, with activities and summaries built into the flow of the text. These features are intended to help readers to grasp, consider and retain the main ideas and arguments of each chapter. The wide margins – in which you will find highlighted the concepts that are key to the teaching – are also intended for student use, such as making notes and points for reflection.

While each book is self-contained, there are a number of references back (and a small number of references forward) to the other books in the series. For those readers who wish to use the books as an exploration in human geography, you will find the references to chapters in the other volumes printed in bold type. This is particularly relevant to the final chapters of Volumes 2–5 as they form a sequence of chapters designed to highlight the uneven character of global development today. On a related teaching point, we have sometimes referred to the group of less developed and developing countries by the term 'third world', in inverted commas to convey the difficulty of continuing to include the diverse range of countries – which embraces some rapidly industrializing nations – under this conventional category. The 'disappearance' of a second world, with the demise of the Communist bloc, also questions the usefulness of the category and, in one way, simply reaffirms the significance of the world's changing geography.

Finally, it remains only to thank those who have helped to shape this Open University course. The names of those responsible for the production of this course are given in the list of Course Team members on page *ii*. Of those, we would like to extend our thanks to a number in particular. It is fair to say that the course would not have had the shape that it does were it not for the breadth of intellectual scholarship provided by our external assessor, Professor Nigel Thrift. Over a two-year period, Nigel, among other activities, commented and offered constructive advice on every draft chapter discussed by the Course Team – in all, some eighty-plus drafts! The Course Team owe him a major debt. We also owe a special debt to our Tutor Panel – Rick Ball, Jenny Meegan and Phil Pinch – for their ceaseless concern that the teaching materials were precisely that: materials which actually do teach. Our editors at the Open University, Melanie Bayley and Fiona Harris, not only raised the professional standard of the series as a whole with their meticulous editing, they also became involved at an early stage in the Course's life and thus were able to smooth the path of its development. Thanks also to Ray Munns for his cartographic zeal and to Paul Smith, our media librarian, who, as ever, translated our vague descriptions of this or that image into an impressive array of illustrations. The typographic design and initial cover idea were developed by Diane Mole who then relinquished the course to Debbie Crouch; their expertise has transformed our typescripts into this handsome series of volumes. The speed and accuracy with which the multiple drafts were turned round by Margaret Charters and Doreen Warwick also deserves our special thanks. Without their excellent secretarial support, the course would not be in any shape at all.

Lastly, in the collaborative style of work by which Open University courses are produced, the awesome task of co-ordinating the efforts of the Course Team and ensuring that the materials are produced to schedule, falls to that of the course manager. It is still a source of amazement to us how our course manager, Christina Janoszka, managed this task as if it were no task at all. We owe her probably more than she is aware.

John Allen
on behalf of
The Open University Course Team

Introduction

Geography has not slipped unnoticed into our lives. Nowadays you do not have to go far to experience the rest of the world. The world, in fact, comes to us in a variety of ways and means: as satellite television images bounced across the globe, as seemingly endless reams of magazines and news print, as styles and fashions which bear the imprint of a dozen countries, or, at the very least, as the food that we eat. The experience does, of course, vary between people and places and in significance and intensity. Perhaps you are largely indifferent to the fact that your European-designed clothing was made in China, but mildly curious about the exotic-looking Caribbean fruits on sale at the local supermarket, and noticeably anxious about the consequences of a radioactive leak at a power station in a nearby country. Yet the more aware we become, however dimly, of what goes on elsewhere having an effect upon our lives, the more we sense the importance of geography.

Underlying this sense of geography is a recognition that much of what happens in our daily lives is increasingly influenced by events beyond our 'local world'. When communications and transport links allow firms to select with the utmost precision where to operate, people in any locality may fear for their jobs and governments worry about what they can and cannot control within their own borders. When all manner of pollution refuses to stop at national frontiers, people take a keener interest in what neighbouring states do with their waste. When supra-national institutions like the European Union add another geographical dimension to our political lives, people start to wonder aloud where government is located. If we wish to understand the local character of our lives, the changing nature of the places in which we live, we have to grasp both the wider, global context of which we are a part and what it is that makes us distinctively local. On the one hand, 'geography' as a concern for the rich variety and changing character of places remains significant; on the other hand, the increasing evidence of geography as a web of global connections should make us even more aware of our place in an interdependent world.

To think about ourselves in this way is to think about the different worlds in which we live. The title of this book, *Geographical Worlds*, in that sense is suggestive of at least two things.

First, and this may seem rather an odd way to express it, we are part of more than one world. We live *local* versions of the world and in so doing we have to locate ourselves within a wider *global* context. We only understand the changes taking place in our own backyard when we begin to understand how changes taking place elsewhere affect our world. We have come to know that our everyday world is shaped by changes in other places. In turn, what happens locally in our world in some way helps to shape the patterns of events and prospects elsewhere. Our worlds are interconnected, however loosely. The world of the 'first world' purchaser of trainers, for example, connects with that of the 'third world' factory worker who makes the shoes, even though the factory worker may go home at night to a world far removed from the global world of finance that exerts power and influence over where she works.

Second, human geography is not only about gaining detailed knowledge of particular places and how they are connected across the globe. It is about understanding and interpreting these local and global worlds. It is about the interpretation and meaning of maps, of travel accounts, of all things environmental – from the social and physical characteristics of the towns and cities in which we live, to the landscapes which frame our world – and so on. Above all, geography contributes a particular slant on the ways in which we understand our place in a changing world. It is this kind of understanding which lies at the heart of what may be called our *geographical imagination*.

o o o o o

The nature of our geographical imagination is one of the central concerns of this book. Over the three chapters, our aim is to introduce what it is to think geographically about the world and our place within it in relation to others. There are a number of aspects to this, all of which appear across the chapters.

The first thing we have come to know about our geographical imagination is that our knowledge of the world and how we make sense of it is always from a certain standpoint, a certain location. We see it from *here*, rather than from *there*. We make sense of our local worlds by looking beyond them, to glean how they differ from elsewhere. In doing so, we gain an understanding of both our part of the world and that of others. We have a sense of what it is like 'here', in a rich, developed country, and what it is like over 'there' in, say, a less developed part of Africa. Or rather, we imagine what it is like from the resources around us: books, maps, television documentaries, radio, talking to others who have travelled there, and the like. Moreover, the effect of 'being here' is more than simply a question of where we find ourselves – where we live, spend time, work and so forth. Who we are and the resources and power we have (or do not have) at our disposal affect the ways in which we picture the world.

Much of what we know about other places is 'made up' in this way, but that does not mean to say that it is wildly inaccurate. It reflects our view of the world – how nature has treated such places, what global influences have shaped them and with what consequences – and may rest alongside accounts of those who are actually in 'other places'. Let us just say for the moment that, in the case of the less developed parts of Africa, those who live 'there' are likely to imagine the world in a number of ways which clash with our interpretation. The uneven nature of global change lends itself to a variety of world views. Quite simply, there is more than one geographical imagination.

Second, as we argue in this book, it is through our geographical imagination that we develop a sense of the global nature of places in which we live; that is, we develop a sense of *how* we are connected, in what ways and to which places. This is not simply about whether or not you have access to a basic telephone line (although for most of the world's population that, too, is not yet a reality); it is about the web of ties and interconnections which appear to make the world a smaller, perhaps more vulnerable place. If we are all 'citizens of planet earth', it is because some people imagine 'one world', a vulnerable globe in a wider cosmos. If the food we eat from hitherto-remote locations and the clothing labels from half way across the globe are markers of this shrinking world, so too is the spread of international tourism and instantaneous communications. In this way, some places once thought of as distant and far apart now appear closer to one another. Our sense of distance in the developed countries, of what is *near* and what is *far*, shapes our view of the world and, along with that, our anxiety over living together in what is seen by many as a small and much-abused planet.

This question of how we understand 'the world as a whole' is a third issue which is grasped through our geographical imaginations. Many of you will no doubt be familiar with old maps of the world which, by today's understanding, only show a small part of the globe or at best a distorted image of a land mass amidst the oceans. Or they show the world in conformity with a mythical or religious vision. From this, we learn that the shape of the world reflects the nature and degree of geographical understanding. The global, in that sense, is what we know and the way that we know it. And this is no less true today than it was two or three or more centuries ago. The contrasting examples of the environmentalists' planet earth, and the world of corporate finance displayed in business advertisements as a series of computer work-stations around the globe, make the point precisely.

Take the issue of globalization, one of the key words of our times. It is often represented as some kind of awesome force or set of forces which is shaping the whole of the contemporary world. Ever-tightening in its network of connections, globalization draws more and more of the globe into one, single world. Take a closer look, however, and there appears to be a number of globalizations, a number of worlds, taking shape. There is the globalization of telecommunications, the globalization of finance, the globalization of culture, and such like. There is also the globalization of environmental concerns, and that of the struggles of indigenous peoples. Moreover, the networks of connections that each lays down do not map one on to the other. Some parts of the world are densely highlighted in some accounts, but not in others. Large tracts of the globe are missed out or skated over in each account, although not necessarily the same locations. In short, there is little point in pretending that we are talking about the *whole* world here. Each 'globalization' is constructing a different world.

Moreover, how each of these worlds is interpreted will depend on your place within it. Again, we are back to local and global worlds and how we grasp the relations between the two.

o o o o o

Geographical Worlds is the first of five volumes in the series *The Shape of the World: Explorations in Human Geography*. Each of the remaining books develops a particular aspect of geographical thinking: on the nature of social space, on nature and the environment, on the meaning of identity of place, and on the very meaning of a global world itself. Each volume raises geographical questions about the world in which we live and offers an insight into the workings of the geographical imagination. In particular, each builds upon the preceding volume in demonstrating how the *uneven geography* of our world is shaped by global processes and, in turn, how such processes work through unevenness to give the world its present and constantly changing shape.

In this volume, our aim is to go no further than to introduce and to stretch your geographical imagination.

John Allen and Doreen Massey

Imagining the world

Chapter 1

by Doreen Massey

1.1 Geographical imaginations

1.1.1 A land-use issue in Honduras

To begin with, read the newspaper cuttings reproduced below which a friend of mine brought back from a trip to Central America.

Land use map presented in congress seeks to affirm Indian rights in the Mosquitia

By ERIC SCHWIMMER

Representatives of the four indigenous groups and native ladinos pose for a photograph during the First Congress on Indigenous Lands of the Mosquitia held this week in the capital. From left to right are Nathan Pravia, a Miskito and project supervisor; Hernán Martínez, a Pech Indian; Jorge Salaverri, representing native ladinos; Ricardo Ramírez, a Garífuna and one of the 21 interviewers; Elmer Waldemar, a Miskito and interviewer; and Isidoro Sánchez, a Tawahka Indian (Photo by Eric Schwimmer)

With the 500th anniversary of Christopher Columbus' discovery of the New World less than three weeks away, the indigenous peoples of the Honduran Mosquitia have reaffirmed their rights to exist, to own their ancestral lands and to use this remote region's natural resources through a unique land use map, which was presented at the First Congress on Indigenous Lands of the Mosquitia held Tuesday and Wednesday in Tegucigalpa.

During two days of lectures, slide shows, presentations and a sampling of the Mosquitia's cultural heritage, the region's four indigenous groups – Miskito, Tawahka-Sumu, Pech/Paya and the Garífuna – and "native" ladinos showed the nation and world that Gracias a Dios department is not an uninhabited region just waiting to be parceled out to all comers, but is extensively used by the Indians to eke out a living, much in the same fashion as their forefathers did prior to the arrival of "Colón."

Moreover, the gathering was used by the Indians to draw up a list of proposals to resolve such delicate questions as land tenure, socio-economic development, conservation, and the rational use of the Mosquitia's natural resources. And taking advantage of the presence of high-level government officials during the congress, the Indians demanded greater social assistance and an end to human rights abuses by omnipotent military authorities based in the region.

BIG SUCCESS

According to Andrew Leake, who together with cultural geographer Peter H. Herlihy of Southeastern Louisiana University headed the project, the congress was a "tremendous success, beyond what I expected."

Leake explained, "I was going to take a few chairs out the night before because I didn't expect that many people to come. We sent out approximately 400 invitations; we started out with 300 then calculated maybe half would come, so then we sent out a further 100 and for both days we've had a full hall.

"And the other factor is people have stayed, and usually in these events they come and then leave very early on." Moreover, he added, "I think the preparations that the Indians have made in terms of what they're going to present resulted in very good short and varied presentations which have kept people's attention."

This latter aspect, he said, was important in creating an "environment within which the politically delicate issue of Indian lands" could be presented objectively.

Leake, whose contract with MOPAWI (Mosquitia Pawisa or Development of the Mosquitia, a non-profit Honduran development organization) expires Dec. 15, described the government's assistance and support for the map project as unprecedented, saying that "every door's opened, everybody has done more than what they should have" including the military, which had representatives present at all times during the two-day meeting.

IMPACT

The map, the central issue of the congress, has already begun to have an impact on the way the government thinks in terms of the Mosquitia's development, said Leake.

"It's already moving people high up in government to rethink their strategies in terms of reserve delimitation, they've copped on to the idea of Indian land use as related to vegetation cover and we're already seeing, just within these two days, people coming up to us to ask us for this information … It's probably the most transcendental event in the Mosquitia's development history which dates back to like 20 or 30 years. It's the first time that … people have been really put on the map."

Another indication of the project's success, he added, is the fact that they have received invitations from Nicaragua, Panama and Paraguay to carry out similar land use mapping projects in those countries – even though the final version of the map still hasn't been published.

This response, he said in modesty, is not just due to their work, but to the "idea that Indians can provide the information which in conjunction with professional, geographic interpretations can generate legitimate maps of Indian land use and the location of Indians."

THE MAP

According to Leake, the idea of preparing a social land use map for the region grew out of the Indians' constant problems with land tenure, and their concern over the destruction of the Mosquitia's natural resources by cattle ranchers, coffee growers and campesinos who assume it has no owners. In addition, Indians had also expressed concern over the granting – by the government – of concessions to foreign firms to exploit wood resources (Stone Container Corp., for example) and to conduct oil exploration.

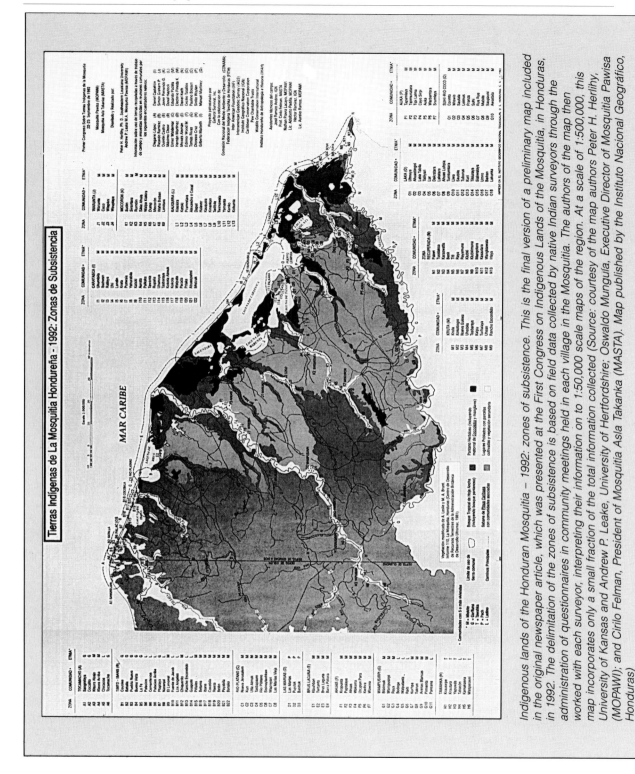

Indigenous lands of the Honduran Mosquitia – 1992: zones of subsistence. This is the final version of a preliminary map included in the original newspaper article, which was presented at the First Congress on Indigenous Lands of the Mosquitia, in Honduras, in 1992. The delimitation of the zones of subsistence is based on field data collected by native Indian surveyors through the administration of questionnaires in community meetings held in each village in the Mosquitia. The authors of the map then worked with each surveyor, interpreting their information on to 1:50,000 scale maps of the region. At a scale of 1:500,000, this map incorporates only a small fraction of the total information collected (Source: courtesy of the map authors Peter H. Herlihy, University of Kansas and Andrew P. Leake, University of Hertfordshire; Oswaldo Munguia, Executive Director of Mosquitia Pawisa (MOPAWI); and Cirilo Felman, President of Mosquitia Asla Takanka (MASTA). Map published by the Instituto Nacional Geográfico, Honduras)

Briefly, the project – conducted by MOPAWI and MASTA (a Mosquito advocacy group) and financed by Cultural Survival and the Interamerican Foundation – consisted of the gathering of information in 22 population centers of the Mosquitia by 21 "interviewers" or "surveyors" who were selected by MOPAWI or democratically chosen by their respective communities and then trained in Puerto Lempira. (One sector, the proposed Tawahka reserve, had already been mapped by Herlihy.)

Traveling on foot, in dug-out canoes or on horse, the interviewers then left for their assigned areas to ask people such questions as where they fish and hunt, where they get the wood to build their homes, and the names of streams, creeks, mountains, lagoons and other geographic landmarks.

After 20 days in the field, the interviewers returned with the preliminary information, which was studied by Leake, Herlihy and others and given to a cartographers of the Instituto Nacional de Geografía to represent it (the information) in the form of a map. Following the preparation of the initial map, the interviewers returned to the field for another 13 days to verify the facts and information obtained from their first visit, and to add anything that was left out.

The result of their work is a map that Leake described as "highly accurate, particularly with place names. The Indians knowledge of place names, particularly on the 1:50,000 map … is very, very precise, and a lot of the points have been cross-checked between two or three different surveyors. We would say it is accurate to 95 percent," he added.

ECOLOGICAL PRESSURES

Aside from presenting the map, the gathering allowed the Indians to express their concern to the public over the continuing deforestation and destruction of the region's varied ecosystems – from pine covered savannahs to tropical broadleaf forest – by "outsiders," local and foreign alike.

Ricardo Ramírez, a Garífuna and one of the 21 surveyors, described the situation in the Río Plátano Biosphere Reserve – a 525,100-hectare protected area covering parts of the departments of Gracias a Dios, Colón and Olancho – as critical.

Due to deforestation, said Ramírez, rivers are drying up and their is heavy erosion, in addition to decreased rainfall.

Other problems, Ramírez said, include the use of explosives to fish by ladinos in the southern part of the Plátano River, and a wanton lack of respect by military authorities – namely the Public Security Force (FSP) – to indigenous peoples.

Police officials, he added, take advantage of the Indians humility and ignorance by levying heavy fines for minor offenses. For example, he said, once a slightly drunk man cried out, for which reason he was arrested by the FSP and then told he must pay a several hundred lempira fine in order to be released.

Moreover, he criticized Bay Islands fishermen, saying they are depleting the region's marine resources by overfishing, without the Mosquitia communities receiving any benefits.

During the information gathering for the map project, he said, some surveyors received death threats from economically powerful persons and large landholders. All that they were offered were "bullets," not "love" and understanding, he concluded.

DEFORESTATION

Speaking for the upper Patuca River region, Soriano Cardona, a Tawahka Indian, blamed cattle ranchers, coffee growers, merchants, campesinos and large landholders for the destruction of that sector's forests, and stressed the importance of land for his people's subsistence.

Moisés Alemán, a Miskito, expressed concern over oil exploration around Ahuas, which could bring further deforestation and, in the event petroleum is discovered, the possibility of oil spills. Moreover, Alemán rapped the quincentenial celebrations, saying that Columbus' discovery of the New

World has only brought indigenous peoples "misery, poverty and contempt."

Describing the Mocorón sector as the "supermarket of wood," Miskito Simón Greham said the inhabitants of the area still feel the effects of the 26,000 Nicaraguan Miskito refugees that received shelter there in the early 1980's during the Nicaraguan Resistance's armed struggle against the Sandinista regime. The refugees, he said, caused extensive damage to the environment, principally deforestation and the destruction of its flora and fauna.

Moreover, Greham said that the zone is being invaded by cattle ranchers who are adding to the deforestation. And equally worrisome, he added, is the intention of the foreign firm Wellington Hall to exploit forest resources along the Warunta River.

With respect to the coastal region, Duval Haylock said fishing boats – which pay no taxes to the department's municipalities – employ large drift nets, taking in enormous quantities of the Mosquitia's marine resources, of which they use only 40 percent.

OFFICIALS PRESENT

Listening to the Indians problems, proposals and demands were high-level government officials, including Vice President Jacobo Hernández Cruz, Defense Minister Flavio Laínez and CONAMA (the National Commission on the Environment) Chairman Dr. Carlos Medina. And attending Wednesday's sessions were President Rafael Leonardo Callejas' sister Melissa and Liberal Party presidential candidate Carlos Roberto Reina, who described the Indians proposals (with respect to the development of the Mosquitia, etc.) as "just" and "logical."

Representatives of the Lencas, an eastern indigenous group, and Nicaraguan Miskitos also attended the congress.

During the latter part of the congress, the participants discussed, drew up and reworded a series of strategies with respect to land tenure, conservation, use of resources and the socio-economic development of the Mosquitia – a

document which they will present to the public and press this week.

Among some of the more important resolutions approved at the congress were:

–   Allow for greater participation of indigenous peoples in the region's development, from the elaboration of proposals for projects to their planning and execution.
–   Require that all projects take into account the region's ethnic diversity.
–   Give women increased participation in development.
–   Require environmental impact studies for all projects.
–   Implement bilingual and bicultural education programs.
–   Take steps to resolve the problem of legalization of Indian lands.
–   Undertake inventories of the region's flora and fauna, of indigenous peoples in this task.
–   Require that oil exploration in the Mosquitia meet with the approval of the Indians.
–   Prohibit the use of the Mosquitia as a toxic waste dump.
–   Ask the government and military to enforce laws against the persons responsible for deforestation and the destruction of animal life (through hunting and commercialization.)
–   Prohibit the colonization of the region by non-indigenous peoples, and relocate colonists in the Río Plátano reserve and the proposed Patuca reserve.

Only time will tell if the Indians achieve their goals, and begin the next 500 years knowing they have the support and understanding of the government and their fellow countrymen, who will hopefully rectify the damage done by Spanish colonizers and their descendents that lead to the extermination of hundreds of thousands of Central American Indians and extensive deforestation – a loss felt by all mankind.

Source: *Honduras This Week*, 26 September 1992, pp. 1, 4, 19

500 years later, indian groups claim their place on map

By WENDY MURRAY ZOBA

The verdict is not yet in as to whether or not the arrival of Cristobal Colón on the shores of the Americas was the boon or bane of these nations. And during this year, the quincentennial "celebration" of his famous or infamous discovery, some native American peoples have decided that it is time to take destiny by the throat.

The four remaining indigenous tribes of Honduras – The Pesch (also known as Paya), the Tawahka-Sumu, the Garífuna (though not "indigenous" in the true sense of the word), and the Miskito – gathered this week for what they hope will be a historic step in indigenous development. The First Congress of Indigenous Peoples of the Mosquitia assembled at the Hotel San Martín on Sept. 22-23 for the purpose of introducing themselves to the nation and to one another, and to unveil the map which they, themselves, have researched and compiled. They hope, as a result, that their motherland and those who orchestrate her business, will get to know them better. Also, that they will remember them in the course of time, when seemingly lucrative business proposals drop into their laps, or when legislation regarding land use and delimitation must fall to the verdict of the powers that be.

These people represent the last vestiges of cultural authenticity, as it existed ante-Columbus. And, though in some cases their Spanish may be broken or their concepts of distance and space somewhat obscure, these are the last of what can be considered truly "Honduran." The First Congress was their moment to speak, explain, and hopefully, be heard regarding who they are and what they are doing with the land and legacy that has been left to them.

HAVE YOU MET ...?
THE MISKITOS

The Miskito Indians have dominated eastern Honduras for centuries and are considered the only true native aborigines of the Mosquitia. They inhabit three zones there, including the savannahs, the coastal plains, and the tropical forests. Descendents of the "Chibcha" are Miskitos who mixed with black slaves along the northern coast during the colonial period when they also came into contact with English and German pirates. They introduced "modern" weapons into the culture of these native peoples, who later used them in pressuring and subduing other smaller Indian groups in the region.

Most Miskitos are bilingual, speaking their native tongue in their homes and villages, and Spanish at school. Depending upon which part of the Mosquitia they inhabit, the Miskitos are known to be excellent horticulturalists, cultivating yuca, bananas, beans, rice and corn. They also breed chickens and depend upon hunting and fishing for daily sustenance.

Numbering between 30,000 and 40,000, their society is well developed and they have expanded into an economically diverse social force. Their coastal lobster industry sometimes brings in as much as Lps. 5 - 10 million a year.

THE GARÍFUNAS

The Garífunas, along with the Miskitos, enjoy a thriving population of some 60,000 to 70,000 scattered along the northern coast of Honduras (with over 2,000 living in the Mosquitia). This group is not truly indigenous, as they were deported to the Bay Islands in 1796 by the British, from the island of Saint Vincent. It seems that these "belligerent" black African slaves were threatening a revolt so the British packed them off to the coastal Islands of Honduras. They soon migrated to the mainland, where they continue to preserve their African culture. The black African slaves mingled with the Island, or Carib, blacks from which has emerged the hybrid culture of the Garífunas.

Fishing in their hand-sewn dug-out canoes continues to provide the main

Garífuna youth may enjoy tropical life [...], but the future of Honduras' Indians hangs in the balance (Photo by Suyapa Carias. A different photograph appeared in the original newspaper article)

source of income and sustenance for this group. But they enjoy an assortment of fresh tropical fruits in their diet, and embellish their cultural history through the preservation of their well known "punta" dancing.

They have been able to maintain a strong ethnic identity and have kept their native language intact (though they speak Spanish as well). Their African heritage is clearly evident in their villages, as their dwellings consist of bamboo and thatched roofing, which sets apart these transplanted members of Honduras' indigenous community.

THE TAWAHKA-SUMU

Neither time nor land space has fared well for this small struggling group located on the lower river banks in the Mosquitia. A generous estimate would put their numbers around 900. However, before Columbus, they flourished along Honduras' eastern border with Nicaragua and probably numbered between 9,000-10,000.

This group felt intense persecution from the Miskitos who were aided by the British in pushing the Tawahka-Sumu inland and westward.

Their native tongue and cultural heritage have been nearly lost, as they have been forced to inter-marry with "mestizos" (mixture of Indians and "ladinos"). They survive today at a subsistence level, hunting and fishing for food on a hand-to-mouth basis, while at the same time living under the constant threat of uncontrolled land penetration and colonization by peasants and cattle ranchers.

THE PESCH (PAYA)

This group once occupied a quarter of the land space in Honduras in pre-Columbian days. However, a population study undertaken in 1982 reflected that the number of Pesch surviving in the Mosquitia at that time was a mere handful.

Today, their numbers are estimated to reach near 2,000. However, only a portion of those could be considered "pure." The Pesch have mixed with both the "ladinos" and the Miskitos, which has resulted in a marked erosion of their ethnic identity and their language.

These people have adopted small scale mining operations – washing gold – as a source of income. Nevertheless, they depend on hand-to-mouth subsistence, harvesting yuca and corn while hunting and fishing. They, along with the Tawahka-Sumu, live under the continual threat of land invasion by ranchers and campesinos.

Source: *Honduras This Week*, 26 September 1992, p. 5

Miskito musician gives congress 'upbeat note'

By ERIC SCHWIMMER

For Elmer Waldemar, a native of the village of Río Plátano and one of the map project's surveyors, the First Congress of Indigenous Lands of the Mosquitia wasn't just giving lectures or explaining the region's problems to participants. It was also an opportunity to show the public the cultural richness of his people through Miskito music and song – a pastime he thoroughly enjoys.

During the few breaks between presentations, Waldemar and fellow Miskitos could often be heard performing songs in their native tongue while strumming guitars and beating tortoise shells, providing an upbeat atmosphere to the event.

Describing his people as humble and fond of their lands and nature, the 27-year old musician said he believes the social land use map will help to show that his people "have a right to our land."

He added, "We are humble, and love our land but we don't like seeing the destruction of so many acres of the (Río Plátano) biosphere's forest. We protect it ... We are agriculturalists, but we are not persons who farm many acres of land, only a little. And with the little we use we are able to feed ourselves."

Waldemar said he interviewed people in seven communities in the Río Plátano district, traveling from one village or hamlet to another on foot or in a dug-out canoe. Wherever he went, he obtained such information as the names of places where Indians hunted, where they fished, the hills where deer roam and how many hours it takes to walk to these places.

Waldemar said his worst experience during the field assignment was a run-in with insects. "I was traveling up river and planned to sleep in a house that didn't have an owner. It was night so I went inside the house, and there were so many mosquitoes there that I couldn't sleep at all and the roof was in ruins," he said laughing.

With respect to the upcoming quincentennial of the New World's discovery by Columbus, Waldeman said his people are neither in favor nor against its celebrations. "For the moment, we only want our lands to be permanent, that is, we love our land, we are fond of the land ... moreover, we are celebrating it (the arrival of Columbus), with this congress," which was "organized to reaffirm our rights to indigenous lands in the Mosquitia."

Source: *Honduras This Week*, 26 September 1992, p. 4

(Note: Typographical errors which appeared in the original versions of these articles have not been corrected here.)

Those cuttings recount part of the story of a battle over what should be the future of a small segment of the earth's surface.

In one sense it is a very 'local' story. Yet it is replicated, in one form or another, day in and day out, over and over again, across the globe. Moreover it raises issues which occur, in battles over places, in all parts of the world. Perhaps, too, at first sight it seems like a simple tale of 'goodies' and 'baddies'. Yet, as I hope to show, it is in fact a good deal more complicated than that, throwing up questions which are by no means easy to resolve.

Moreover, this battle over land in coastal Honduras raises a range of issues which go to the heart of 'geography'. For this is the story of a struggle over how space, place and nature are to be understood. Those three terms – space, place and nature – are central to a geographical understanding of the world. And yet, as the Honduran story indicates, the different participants had quite contrasting views of each of them.

Finally, the story is also fascinating from a geographical point of view because central to the way in which the debate was fought out was one of geography's most characteristic tools of analysis – the map. Or actually, of course, two maps. For at the heart of the case was the conflicting evidence of two very different maps, each in some sense of the same place, yet each representing a distinctive understanding of that place and of its resources.

Let us investigate a little further.

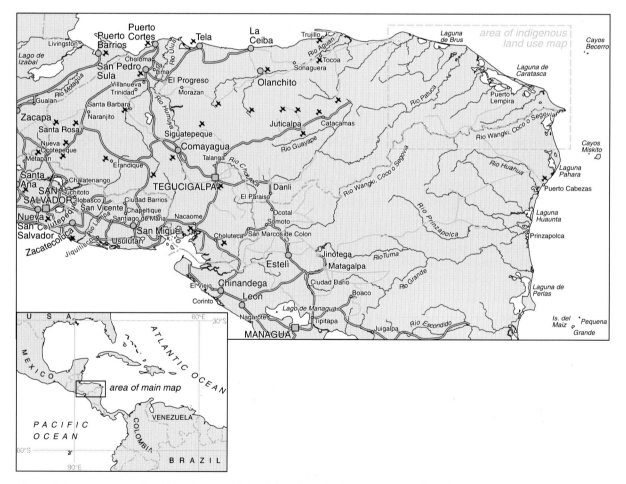

Figure 1.1 Honduras – the kind of map which might otherwise have been used: notice how 'empty' the Mosquitia is

1.1.2   Some questions: place, nature, space

Let us start off by confronting some of the big issues raised by this case. There are three main bundles of questions. The *first* revolves around the question of what rights particular groups of people have to lay claim to places (that is, parts of the earth's surface). The *second* set of issues raises similar problems in relation to resources and the environment. *Thirdly*, there are questions about the basic geography – the interpretation of this space on the earth's surface – and the contrasting ways in which it is seen by the different protagonists.

First, then, there is the question of what rights particular groups of people have to lay claim to places, and what kind of claims might be considered legitimate.

contested views of place

Activity 1   Before you read on, consider what your own reactions were as you read through the cuttings. These will be your immediate reactions, and they may well change or become more complex as you consider things further. Don't worry about that. For the moment just jot down your initial ideas.

For instance:

o   Whose place is this?

o   Does it belong to 'local people', or do people who arrive later have a right to it as well?

If you find these questions difficult to answer, well and good!

One immediate reaction might be that the place belongs to the people who have always been there. This is the kind of argument one hears, not only in battles of this sort where indigenous groups face multinational corporations and cattle-ranchers, but also in confrontations which are perhaps less stark – where the rural village 'locals' in a first world country resist the encroachment of a new, modern development – and in confrontations which may bring out antipathy between social groups – where existing residents resist the arrival of migrants, for instance. So, as we investigate the case of Honduras, keep in the back of your mind that the issues and questions it raises apply also to debates and battles reported daily in newspapers all over the world: indeed, in some of which you may be involved yourself.

local people

How, then, can we evaluate the argument that a place belongs to 'the locals', to the people who have always been there? Here in coastal Honduras this apparently simple principle is in fact full of problems.

To begin with, *none* of the participants in this debate are 'locals' in the sense that they have always lived in that place. The Garífunas hail from the other side of the Atlantic Ocean, from Africa whence they were brought by the British as slaves to St Vincent. Having threatened rebellion against their treatment by the British, they were deported in 1796 to the Bay Islands off the Honduran coast. It was from there that, finally, they migrated to this place which is in dispute. Even the Miskitos, the group to which the second article refers as 'the only true native aborigines', arrived, originally, from elsewhere. Although these articles do not say so, it is known from other sources that the first occupants of the continent we now know as America arrived by crossing over from northern Asia by what we now call the Bering Strait. This, of course, happened thousands of years ago (at least 15,000 years ago) but the point at issue is one of principle: that we are all, somewhere in our long historical pasts, the products of migration. 'The locals' are not people who have always been here; rather, they are just the people who arrived here first, or who have been here longest.

Let us, then, at least for the moment, accept that definition of the local people of this place. But then another issue arises. For although each of the indigenous groups has been here many centuries, none of them is of purely local provenance. What I mean by this is that each of the groups is already a mixture of local and non-local influences. The very character of each of them is already a product, in part, of contacts with the world beyond this local place. Thus, as I have already mentioned, the Garífunas trace their very history back to Africa. Moreover, centuries later as they live in coastal Central America, and as the second article states, 'they continue to preserve their African culture. The black African slaves mingled with the Island, or Carib, blacks from which has emerged the hybrid culture of the Garífunas. ... They have been able to maintain a strong ethnic identity and have kept their native language intact (though they speak Spanish as well). Their African heritage is clearly evident in their villages, as their dwellings consist of bamboo and thatched roofing, which sets apart these transplanted members of Honduras' indigenous community.' The Miskitos, too, considered the most aboriginal of the groups, have over the centuries mixed with black slaves and come into contact with English and German pirates. Such contacts introduced new elements into the existing culture. At least some of the people, as the newspaper stories indicate, have Spanish names, or names like Elmer Waldemar. Finally, both the Tawahka-Sumu and the Pesch (or Paya) have lost much of their former cultural heritages and languages and have interbred with other indigenous groups, with ladinos (Indian–Spanish mix) and with mestizos (Indian–ladino mix). None of this implies that there is nothing left which is particular to the cultures of these groups. Indeed, the final cutting reports on the music which was an integral part of the congress, and the presentation of which was seen as 'an opportunity to show the public the cultural richness of his people through Miskito music and song'. The point is not that the cultural uniqueness of these groups has been lost, but that it is in every case the product of some kind of historical mixing – it is

hybrid culture   what the newspaper calls 'hybrid'.

So far, then, in this first bundle of issues, we have managed to problematize (to complicate by asking difficult questions of) the whole notion of 'local people'. But let us say that in this particular case we can come to an agreement about who they are (even if we can only call them 'local' after hedging the term about with a number of reservations). In coming to this agreement about who they are, the next stage in the enquiry then concerns the nature of the claims they are making.

The claim which the indigenous groups are making about this place is for some kind of exclusivity. Their own history contains episodes of invasion and displacement. In the past, the Miskitos have (with British help) subdued non-Miskito groups including some of their current allies such as the Tawahka-Sumu. Yet today one of their claims is against the right of subsequent 'invasion'. Specifically they seek to 'Prohibit the colonization of the region by non-indigenous peoples, and [to] relocate colonists'. They have a notion of '"outsiders", local and foreign alike'. What do you think of this? What rights do people who arrive in a particular part of the earth's surface earlier than others have to exclude the entry, even to throw out, people who would arrive later? This is not an easy question to answer. Moreover, it becomes even more difficult when the question is extended beyond this particular case. Do people in the richer countries of the world have the right to deny entry to those from poorer countries? (Here we meet a further central concept in geography – uneven development – which will be considered in Chapter 3.)

The *second* major bundle of questions relates to this. These concern issues of resources and of people's relationship to nature and the environment.

contested views of nature

The central question at issue in this debate is what should be the future for this part of the world. What kinds of developments – in particular, economic developments – should be allowed? Let us take for further analysis the contrast between the two most starkly opposed views of the future: on the one hand that of the indigenous people and on the other hand that of the companies and cattle-ranchers who wish to move into the area. (There are also peasant farmers moving into the region.) Each of these two possible futures is based on its own distinctive understanding of nature and the environment. The two contending visions involve radically different relationships to, and uses of, 'the natural world'.

On the one hand, if the developers get their way there will be deforestation and the planting of large areas of crops. Roads will be built, to open up the area. To the wood, and oil, and beef and coffee companies this area is a potential source of resources. Not only will their exploitation produce profits for the companies, but also these are resources very much in demand by people in other parts of the world. To exploit them in the most 'efficient' manner possible would indeed be the most rational use of these resources.

Note, however, that the very first article in this set of cuttings talks *both* of the indigenous people eking out a living 'much in the same fashion as their forefathers did prior to the arrival of "Colón"' (Cristobal Colón, by the way, is the person who in English is known as Christopher Columbus) *and* of those groups' claim to preserve 'the rational use of Mosquitia's natural resources'. Clearly, what is the most rational use depends on your understanding of nature and of how it should be used. The indigenous people's way is to live in a highly varied and mixed relation to nature. Even the scale and form of organization varies: from subsistence and gathering from the wild, to small-scale farming, to the one quite sizeable enterprise which is mentioned, that of coastal lobster-fishing. The range of products derived is impressive: yuca, bananas, beans, rice, corn, chickens, fish, gold, lobster, other fresh and tropical fruits: indeed, one journalist says that the groups were precisely concerned to underline the varied nature of the region's ecosystems – 'from pine covered savannahs to tropical broadleaf forest'. The underlying theme is of indigenous 'land use as related to vegetation cover'.

In this context, what the indigenous people argue is that the expansion of activities such as cattle-ranching, lumber-production and coffee-growing will destroy that varied ecosystem and thus their ability to live as they do. In particular, they are concerned about deforestation, which can lead to soil erosion and the drying-up of rivers, as well as destroying resources the indigenous people already use. They are also worried about the possibility of oil spills.

In the broadest of terms, the indigenous people would probably argue that they live in a harmonious relation to nature, while some of those who wish to develop the area in other ways will cut across that relationship. Both local people and incomers, however, see nature – in so far as we can tell from these cuttings – primarily as a resource. They just disagree about how to use that resource. And yet, every now and then there is a hint of another side of things, as some of the local representatives speak of the love they have for their lands and for nature, and of their desire to protect it for itself.

The point is, and to link up now with the first bundle of issues, that the case which the indigenous people are making is not only that 'they got here first', but that in the centuries over which they have been in this place they have evolved a way of life which is integrally related to the character of the area. It is not just their occupation of the land which is at issue but the fact that the entry of new people, new activities and – crucially – different views of the world, will prevent them from going on living in the way that they have known for so long.

Activity 2 What do you think of this argument? Before you answer, or while you think about your answer, consider also other situations in which a parallel question might arise. What, for instance, of the residents of an exclusive, upper-class suburb up in arms against a plan to build low-cost housing in the area: 'It would destroy the whole area and the way we are used to living within it'.

Maybe you think there are differences between the cases. If so, what are they?

the local and the global

One possible reply to these arguments is that this cannot be seen as just a 'local' issue. What is at issue is in fact a highly complex conflict over resources which is *both* local *and* global. While, seen from one perspective, this is a case which concerns the survival (or not) of locally distinct cultures and ways of living, seen from another perspective it is a conflict over access to the world's resources. The companies and others who wish to move in might well argue, as they point to figures showing an impending crisis, the ever-growing shortage of resources to sustain the world's population, that a group of local people does not have any legitimate right to deny access to the world's diminishing supply. Indeed, the customers who buy the oil and the beef, in the silence of their (our?) continuing consumption are implicitly supporting this argument.

And yet, there is another way of thinking globally which might lead to the opposite conclusion. On the whole, it is probably the case that the people to whom these commodities will be sold are already richer and have higher standards of living (in the way those things are usually measured) than the people whose lives are likely to be disrupted by their production. The resource demands of the potential consumers are greater than those of the local people. So the question could be turned back to the incomers, in the query as to whether they have the right to disrupt local, and relatively poorer local, economies in order to serve the demands of other, richer, people who live elsewhere. Maybe 'the problem of resources' demands a response from the lifestyles of consumers rather than, or as well as, the lifestyles of those in areas where production will take place. Even 'thinking globally' can be done in different ways. What is raised here is the fact that this is an issue not just of abstract geography (local/global) but of the relationship between that geography and the already existing, and unequal, distribution of power and resources.

There is another way, too, of seeing that intimate connection between geography and power. Consider for a moment the geography of resources required to sustain the lifestyles of the different social groups in this story. Those waiting, in the first world or in the cities of the third world, to consume the wood and oil and beef and coffee probably draw on much of the globe for the range of resources necessary to support their standard and style of living. One question which could be asked is whether the Miskitos and the Garífunas make similar, reciprocal, demands. I am sure there are 'Western' trucks and cigarettes and other goods in the villages of coastal Honduras, but broadly speaking the sources of the resources required to maintain their lives are relatively local, certainly by comparison. The indigenous groups imply this way of thinking about the issue when one of their number refers – ironically – to a part of the area as a 'supermarket of wood'. Should some areas of the world function as 'supermarkets' for others? When companies and consumers argue that we need to recognize the 'globalization' of supply and demand, the globalization of the market, it is necessary also to consider how contrastingly placed are different social groups in relation to this globalization.

The *third* issue will just be briefly indicated here. It is that, just as nature/the environment was understood in different ways by the different protagonists in this affair, so also was space itself. Even the way in which the place is measured differs between the two main approaches. Even the views of distance start from different practices and different presumptions. One of the articles says that the indigenous people's concepts of distance and space are 'somewhat obscure', yet it is clear from the whole account that there is strong agreement on the geography of the area among the people interviewed during the preparation of the new map. It is not a question of lack of knowledge, but of *a different kind of knowledge*. The indigenous peoples think of space, and measure distance, in terms of their practical relation to this place. Distances, for instance, are measured in terms of 'how many hours it takes to walk to these places'. The government officials and the companies, by contrast, think in terms of systems of measurement which are based neither in knowledge of that particular locale nor in experience of living in it. For them, there are units of measurement – such as hectares and kilometres – which reflect their own geography. While the indigenous groups' main concern is the integration of the land into the rhythm of their daily lives, the concerns of government and of the companies spread far wider. They need units of measurement which will enable them to compare this area – its extent, its 'development potential', the distance to markets far away – with other areas elsewhere. Their way of thinking about space, in abstract generalizable units, reflects both the geography and the power of their interests.

contested views of space

1.1.3 Making maps

The issues, then, are complex, but what is of interest to us at this moment is that they are being fought out, quite centrally, through *maps*. The new social land use map drawn up by the indigenous people is the centrepiece of the proceedings of the congress. It is the means by which they feel they can enter the debate over the future of this region.

Let us then explore a bit further this issue of maps.

To begin with, and the most important point of all, there are *two* maps, and they are different. Each of them presents a different understanding of the region. Indeed, the whole *point* of the indigenous people's map is to present an alternative to the 'normal' one, expressed perhaps in the 'development-plan' map of the government or the companies. The aim for the indigenous people, when drawing up their own map, was above all to register their own presence in the region. Their map 'showed the nation and world that Gracias a Dios department is not an uninhabited region'. Foremost among the things that they wanted to put on their map, therefore, were the names of the indigenous communities – well over a hundred are listed in the legend. And against each name is registered the name of the group which lives there. Also marked are the zones of subsistence (*zonas de subsistencia*) on which each group of settlements draws for its livelihood. Indigenous names for the rivers and lagoons are given as well – and the articles imply that many more names have been collected during the research.

Now, the reason the groups feel they have to present this information is that they are not on the maps which are usually used in considering the future of the region. Neither they themselves nor the uses they make of the area appear. Moreover, they argue, their absence from the map is important. It has effects. If people think the area is uninhabited they might see it as 'just waiting to be parceled out to all comers'. (Of course, another view of nature, which valued the persistence of 'wilderness', might well object that even so-called 'empty land' should not be understood as unrestrictedly available for exploitation and development. 'Nature' need not be thought of simply as natural resources.) The indigenous people speak of the constant problems they have over land tenure 'and their concern over the destruction of the Mosquitia's natural resources by cattle ranchers, coffee growers and campesinos [peasants] *who assume it has no owners*' (my emphasis). One can imagine the scene, say in the development office of a lumber company, outside this region and maybe not even in Honduras. A group of company executives stands around a table and peer down at the map laid out before them. This act in itself may make the place seem very vulnerable, to their eyes and to their plans. But what makes the situation even worse, from the point of view of the indigenous groups, is that they are not even on that map! It is easy to imagine how much simpler it must be to plan – to cut down the forest here, to open up a plantation there, build a road across this way – if there is no trace, as the pointers are wielded and the lines are drawn, of the density of settlement and use of this place by those who are already living there. So, the new map is designed to make others see, and understand, the place differently.

representation

maps as social products

The more general lesson we can take away from this episode is that *maps are means of representation* and every individual map embodies a particular way of understanding, a particular interpretation of the place it is depicting. What this means is that maps are 'social products' (we shall return to this point later). Their design – for instance, what they include and what they omit – reflects different experiences, priorities and interpretations. As we see in this case, just putting things on to a map can be empowering (in the same way as omitting them can be disempowering). The phrase we so often use of 'putting something on the map' is not an idle one. Indeed, it is used in the newspaper articles. And the particular interpretation which a map adopts helps to endow a place with that meaning.

Note also how important it was to the indigenous groups to *name* things on the map, and to name them in their own tongues. The new map laid great stress on this process of the naming, in their own languages, of streams, lagoons, mountains and other physical landmarks. The accuracy of local place names was of great importance.

Box 1.1 A problem of naming

This issue of naming confronted *me* when I began to write about this case. What should I call the area, the broad area, in which it was set? 'Honduras' is probably a name which means little in relation to these people's history – certainly it is not their name even if they think in terms of a unit which conforms to it. In an effort to avoid mention of nation states I thought of using 'Central America', but of course that is just as bad – the word 'America' was only coined after Columbus' voyage: it derived from Amerigo Vespucci, one of the early European arrivals. I used Honduras, because I thought that might mean most to a general audience today. But I hope you can appreciate the difficulty, and also see that it points towards a much more general – and very major – issue: the power of naming things on maps.

As we can see from all this, maps can reflect the power of the people who draw them up. The 'normal' maps – effectively the dominant ones – were probably drawn up in university, government and company departments. They reflected the view of the world from those locations, and thereby reinforced these already powerful perspectives on the region. For the indigenous people, the reports say, their own map gave them a sense of their right to exist, to own their 'ancestral lands', to use the natural resources. It confirmed them as legitimate sources of information about the area.

My use of the term 'legitimate' here is quite deliberate. Indeed, this term is used by Andrew Leake, one of the people who helped draw up the map. He refers to the 'idea that Indians can provide the information which in conjunction with professional, geographic interpretations can generate legitimate maps of Indian land use and the location of Indians'. The indigenous people, in other words, already possessed great knowledge of the area. But it was a different kind of knowledge, and in a different form, from that of the people they were seeking to impress. What they needed help with was translating this knowledge into a form (a map) which their audience would recognize and appreciate as 'legitimate'.

Finally, maps can also help give access to power. Indeed, this was what the whole exercise was about. Because for the indigenous people producing their map was a way of saying they knew their area, even of asserting their existence, the hope was that they would thereby gain the right to participate in discussions over the future of the region. Without their alternative map, their alternative geography, the future of the place might be different. The way we imagine the world matters: it has effects.

Maps, then, are our own creations. They express particular interpretations of the world, and they affect how we understand that world and how we see ourselves in relation to others. They are also, perhaps, one of the most distinctively 'geographical' ways of depicting, or imagining, the world and places within it.

1.1.4   Other ways of imagining the world

However, maps are by no means the only way of depicting the world. There are many other means by which we come to build our understanding of the geography of the world about us. Some of these ways are quite specialized (we might think, perhaps, of academic geographical writing) but many of them are part of our everyday lives.

Think, for instance, of *travel brochures*. These are important means by which we get to know about places other than our own. They are, however, both produced for a particular purpose and usually read by us with a certain set of questions in mind. They are produced in order to entice us to take a holiday there and as we read them we judge the view of the place presented against our mental checklist of requirements for the kind of holiday we want this year. Of course the place, *and the view of the place which is presented*, will depend on the type of holiday on offer.

Many travel brochures for the Algarve in southern Portugal, for instance, concentrate on promoting the sun/sea/sand-and-golfing kind of holiday. The brochures are full of deep blue skies and people with suntans, of white villas and gleaming hotels, of drinks on the terrace and golf in the evening sunlight. And this is, indeed, what we want to know about as we thumb through, wondering if we can really afford to go abroad this year. Now, this is not an *incorrect* view of this part of Portugal. But clearly, like any other portrait, it does not tell the whole story. I remember being in the Algarve in 1974, when the whole country was caught up in revolution. I stood in one of those seaside towns and saw soldiers in the back of a truck cheering happily at the changes going on. Everywhere there were posters, particularly one of a rifle with a red carnation in its barrel. The Algarve, with its population of small-holding farmers and fishermen was an important base for a Maoist form of revolution (whereas, over the mountains to the north, in the Alentejo, the Communist Party was more important).

The travel brochure says nothing of this. It is not its purpose to do so. Yet those events of the mid-1970s are still important in this region: they live on in the minds and memories as part of the reality of this place in the imaginations of its inhabitants as they continue to farm or fish, or to work as a waitress, hotelier or casino attendant in the area's booming tourist industry. What we see as the place from the tourist brochure is unlikely to be the same as that which an inhabitant would describe. All views are partial. And what is important is to remember that fact.

Some partial views, moreover – some interpretations from a particular perspective – may be legitimately open to criticism, perhaps because of the effects they may induce. The tourist-brochure understanding of the Algarve, for instance, barely mentions the local people, except perhaps for some ritual mention of their remarkable friendliness. The problem with this is that it presents the place as simply something to be enjoyed by tourists. We are insulated from the daily lives of the local people – indeed, from the effect (good or bad) that tourism may be having on those lives. Not only are we deprived of a whole range of knowledge (unless we take the trouble to go to the library, say, and search out other kinds of information), but we are also removed from the responsibility of thinking about what effect our holidays might be having.

The selective understanding presented by the tourist brochure has exactly the same kind of effect on us as the absence of the Miskitos and the Garífunas from the maps of coastal Honduras had on the commercial lumber companies planning a new plantation. As our imaginary company directors draw their lines across the Mosquitia, so we plan our next trip to sun, sea and sand.

Another everyday way in which we all build up our *geographical imaginations* is through *news reports*. Those reports of events in far-away places are an important part of the way in which we construct pictures of the world and give meaning to them. Moreover, and this is the really important point, it is argued by people working in the field of 'geopolitics' (that is, the geographical aspects of politics, particularly at an international level) that this process of building up particular ways of interpreting the world is an important aspect of politics itself.

geographical
imagination

This is a difficult, and perhaps unexpected, point so let us examine it through two examples.

During the so-called Cold War the two sides were classically referred to in the English-speaking media as the West and the Communists. Think about those terms: what do you notice about them? For one thing, they are not symmetrical. One side is called by a geographical direction on the compass (West), the other by its dominant ideological affiliation (Communism). Sometimes, of course, the terms West and East were used, but that had difficulties because 'the West' in fact includes many countries which are in the East in geographical terms – Japan being chief among them. But it was only very rarely indeed that the West was called by a name that brought to mind *its* ideological/political affiliation, or its mode of economic organization. While the Communist world was called communist the West was very rarely called capitalist. The effect of this, it is argued, is while drawing attention to the communist characteristics of the enemy, to leave our own characteristics unexamined. Moreover, when those characteristics *were* alluded to directly it was usually in the very positive name 'the free world'. Here again we can see how important it can be to have the power over giving names to parts of the world.

A second example could be the Gulf War of 1991, which followed from Iraq's invasion of Kuwait in 1990. It was a war, as has often been said, which was played out day by day, even minute by minute, on the news media. We could 'actually see what was going on'. The bombing of Baghdad and of the Iraqi army by the Allies was on a very considerable scale. How was it, people have asked, that so many people seem to have accepted this with such equanimity? Leaving aside the issue of whether or not it was justified, it was a major campaign which resulted in a major loss of Iraqi lives. And yet there was an apparently easily won majority support from the people of the countries involved. One argument which has been put forward is that Iraq as a place had been quite deliberately portrayed in a particular way. Among other things, it was often portrayed as somehow an empty place with one major town (Baghdad), and occasionally some smaller ones, set in miles upon miles of inhospitable – and uninhabited – desert. In fact, of course, Iraq is a rapidly 'modernizing' economy, with a highly complex society and a history which stretches back to include some of the so-called cradles of our own civilization: Babylon and the long crescent valley between the Tigris and the Euphrates. This was Mesopotamia. However, it has been argued, had we been more aware of this immense social complexity, and reality, of present and past, the massive bombing of this country might have given more people more pause for thought. As it was, Iraq was constructed in our geopolitical imaginations in a very different way, in order to have very different effects.

One final example. But this time spend a few minutes thinking about images yourself, before reading on.

Activity 3 The third world. What images come into your mind as you consider that term? Pause a moment and jot down a few things.

Now, it may well be that, when you stopped to think about it, the images which 'the third world' called to mind were quite complicated; there may even have been quite a few of them, which cross cut and even perhaps contradicted each other. It is often that way; we quite frequently hold a bundle of different images of the same place, drawing on one or other of them as may be most appropriate to the situation in hand.

So let us concentrate on particular questions. Would you say the images which came into your mind – your geographical imagination of the third world – were characterized by vulnerability or strength?

Activity 4 Examine your geographical imagination a little further. Which characteristic in each of the following pairs of characteristics would you say most accurately captures your bundle of images of the third world? Tick the one in each pair which most applies:

strength   vulnerability
passivity   activity
a hand stretched out for aid   people at work

I focus on these characteristics for a reason. Over recent years there has been considerable debate, particularly amongst people working in aid agencies, about the most appropriate images to use in appeals for aid. It is sometimes argued that the most successful images in terms of bringing in donations are those which show people suffering, or directly supplicating. We see so many such pictures: people crowded in refugee centres, waiting in line for water or food, the close-ups concentrating on little children and on women or old people. There is no question that such pictures are very moving.

But it has also been argued both that these images give a false picture of the situation and that they thereby do little to help in the longer run. Too often, it is argued, the dominant representation is of passivity – people standing around, waiting in line. The images may even be exploitative, or may actively work to sentimentalize the situation: one thinks of the numerous pictures of beautiful, suffering young women with a baby at their breast. Would it not be better, it is asked, to picture people *doing* things, getting on with their lives, planning and working for survival? Would it not be better to show people as strong? Not only would such pictures be closer to the reality of most parts of the world in receipt of such aid, but the image also changes, in a sense, 'the analysis'. Here are not people standing with their hands outstretched but people working hard in a highly unequal world. Such a different picture might even alter our opinion of what might be done about the lines of inequality which structure the world economy. It is as a result of this kind of debate that a number of charities have produced 'guidelines' for the kinds of representation deemed to be acceptable.

Save the Children recognises that communicating its work in non-discriminatory ways is fundamental to the values and principles it holds and the effectiveness of its Equal Opportunities Policy.

Save the Children aims to ensure that its communications and appeals use:

accurate representation of Save the Children's work, which reflects the organisation's principles, values and practice in respect of the Rights of the Child charter and its Equal Opportunities Policy.

images or words which do not damage the dignity of the children/adults with whom Save the Children works.

strong messages that do not trivialise, distort or misrepresent the work of Save the Children.

△ The vast majority of overseas staff are employed from the countries where Save the Children works. Images of "dominant" white project workers dispensing aid to "passive" villagers contradict Save the Children's way of working in partnership.

The images and text used in all communications must be accurate and should avoid stereotypes and cliches.

Text and images selected solely for shock value can trivialise, distort or misrepresent the work of Save the Children. To evoke concern and stimulate interest and action, present facts and photographs accurately.

△ People in developing countries play an active role in development as shown by these villagers stacking millet ears they have grown in Mali, one of the three poorest countries in the world.

images are everybody's business

Clips from Save the Children's Focus on Images, *emphasizing the importance of images*

Summary of section 1.1

o   There are many forms of geographical imagination: maps, travel brochures, travel writing, news reports and appeals for aid are just a few of these. (You might list some more for yourself.) All of these are ways in which we come to have an understanding of the world.

o   All of them, also, are products of society and will reflect the power and the interests, the viewpoint, of the group or groups which drew them up.

o   Three of the key concepts in a geographical understanding of the world are: place, space and nature. But each of these may be understood in different ways by different groups of people.

1.2   The shape of the world

1.2.1   Picturing the world

Maps are a particular way of representing the world in which we live. Like all other forms of such representation, they are means of locating ourselves in, and finding our way about in, a larger context. They are a way of making sense of complexity and of helping us get a grip on where we are.

This may seem only too obvious, but I mean it in a much deeper sense than, say, the fact that a town map, for instance, will give you a sense of the city you are visiting, or that a road map will help you drive from Birmingham to Barcelona. Maps, as we saw in the last section, are always the product of particular societies and particular groups of people. They reflect specific ways of thinking; each is designed to serve a specific purpose. At its simplest, no map can show everything – to do so it would have to be as big as, indeed absolutely the same as, the world it represents. So things have to be omitted. And that process of selection tells us something about the society which produced the map. On British Ordnance Survey maps, for instance, churches are shown, with their own special symbol, but mosques are not. But it is also more than this: for maps also reflect ways of thinking. They provide an insight into how the people who produced them imagine the world in which they live and how they place themselves within it. It is that which we are going to explore briefly now.

Plate 1 is a map of the world. It is the map of the world of a particular people with a particular way of thinking. It is also one of the oldest surviving world maps, and it consists of an impression on a clay tablet, just five inches by three. Have a look at it before we go on.

This map was made two and half thousand years ago by the Babylonians (in present-day Iraq). It is, apparently, straightforward in design. Two lines, which probably represent the Tigris and Euphrates rivers, run down the map across the flat, circular earth; in the very central circle are Babylon and other important cities; and surrounding all these is the circular 'Bitter River' across which, it seems, lived legendary beasts (Berthon and Robinson, 1991, p. 12). Let us, for the moment, note just two points about this map.

First, it inaugurates a tradition which has characterized many maps through the ages, which is that the people who design the map place themselves and/or their most important symbolic place right in the centre. In this case it is Babylon, located at the centre of the world.

The second point, however, is not evident from just examining the map. Examination of the map alone, with no other knowledge of the society within which it was produced, might lead us to suppose that its design reflected the state of scientific knowledge of the time. However, this would be to interpret this map in the terms of our own times. For in fact the Babylonians were 'scientifically' very advanced. As Berthon and Robinson write:

This crude picture of the world seems a disappointing memento of a civilization which was in many other respects so brilliant. The Babylonians were, for example, superb astronomers. Their figures on the motions of the sun and moon reveal only three times the margin of error of nineteenth-century astronomers armed with powerful telescopes. Yet when it came to picturing the world and the structure of the universe, science was thrown to the winds ...

(Berthon and Robinson, 1991, p. 12)

In other words, this map reflects the fact that, although the Babylonians were in our terms scientifically advanced, scientific thought was not dominant in forming their broad outlook on the world. What was more important was the religious structure of the universe. The Babylonians believed that, beneath the flat disc of the earth was a subterranean sea, called the Apsu, which, through its patron god Enki, or Ea, provided the river valley above with the water which allowed the plants to flourish. Above the earth other gods held court, while the earth itself was the domain of the god Enlil. It was this account of their world, rather than their astronomical observations and measurements, which was drawn upon in the construction of this map of the world in about 500 BC.

Such religious constructions can also be found in maps made in the Christian world. The *mappae mundi* are perhaps the clearest example. These maps – like the famous *mappa mundi* in Hereford cathedral – were pictures of the world which embodied the stories of Christianity. One of the most impressive of them is shown in Plate 2. As Harley writes: 'Such world maps ... used to be discussed by geographers for their lack of realism. But today we read the Ebstorf map as a Christian metaphor in which time and space are indivisible' (Harley, 1990, p. 11). As he explains, it is a picture of God in which the world is shown as the body of Christ. Christ's head can be seen at the top of the map (which is, in contrast to our convention, the east). To the left of Christ's head is the Garden of Eden, at his feet at the bottom (west) appears Gibraltar 'and his hands reach out north and south to embrace the circular earth in a gesture of salvation' (Harley, 1990, p. 11). It is this weaving of a story, that of Christ's life and relation to the world, which is being referred to when Harley writes, in the quotation above, about time and space being indivisible. This is very different from our own current notions where a map gives a picture of a piece of space at a particular moment in time, thus effectively separating the spread of space from the passage of time.

There is another similarity, too, between the Ebstorf map and the Mesopotamian. For neither of them represent a simple history of gradually increasing scientific knowledge. In the Mesopotamian case the map did not make use of the scientific information at its immediate disposal. In the case of the *mappae mundi* a whole body of scientific knowledge had been 'forgotten'. The Greeks had what we would think of as a far more scientific understanding of the world than is displayed in these medieval Christian maps. Claudius Ptolemy had written his *Geographia* in the second century AD. It is an amazing book (available as Ptolemy, 1991), which takes a very mathematical approach to cartography. The society in which Ptolemy moved recognized the earth to be a sphere, and the maps in his atlas contain conical projections (see Plate 3) and calculations of latitude and longitude. But Ptolemy's work was largely forgotten for a thousand years, as Europe entered a period when religious views held sway. As Berthon and Robinson put it, 'Religion versus science was the great wrestling match of early Christian thinkers' (Berthon and Robinson, 1991, p. 48). The *mappae mundi* represent to a large extent the victory of the former over the latter when it came to picturing the world.

But when Ptolemy's work was once again unearthed it rapidly became the model for a new cartography (Harley, 1990, p. 23). And it was no accident that this other way of looking at the world was seen to be more important than the religious. Portolan charts for navigation, so important to exploration and the search for resources, had been challenging the dominance of the religious view of the globe:

Ptolemy's Geographia *cannot be assessed solely in a humanistic or scientific light. Its knowledge, a new systematic device for controlling the world, was appropriated by the power-brokers of fifteenth-century Europe. Though the 1472 manuscript was commissioned for his personal library by Federico di Montefeltro, Duke of Urbino, other copies were made as diplomatic gifts. Finely illuminated manuscripts were a fitting status symbol but they also helped those of high rank to visualize their territorial ambitions. Ptolemy was welcomed. Pope Pius II was to award the* Geographia *the official Vatican stamp of approval (*nihil obstat*) on doctrinal grounds.*

Hints of this geopolitical role are found in the manuscripts of the Geographia. *Many contain a miniature picture of the first translator – Jacopus Angelus – presenting a copy of his work completed in 1409 to Pope Alexander V. The dedication is more revealing, expressing a hope that the book would serve as 'an announcement of his coming rule ... so that he may know what vast power over the world he will soon achieve.'*

Prophetic words: on a later world map, armed with demarcations of longitude, another pope would divide the New World first revealed by Columbus. The geographical grid rediscovered with Ptolemy would become an instrument of partition. On a paper world ruled by geometry this was an easy task.

(Harley, 1990, p. 24)

It could not be clearer. On the one hand, interpretations of the world, and their representation in maps, may change in response to circumstances. On the other hand, those circumstances are rarely 'neutral'. The map will be related to the current balance of power or to a bid to change that balance. It is exactly what is happening in coastal Honduras, in the Mosquitia, today.

Christopher Columbus, too, had a copy of a 1490 edition of the *Geographia*. No landmass lay between the western shores of Europe and the eastern coast of Asia.

In fact, of course, a whole continent lay there. And across that continent a whole range of societies had developed their own ways of mapping the world. Sometimes these representations of the space of life were communicated through dance or through gestures or through festivals, and much of this has been lost. But other maps existed in a form akin to that which was known in Europe. And once again the maps each represented a particular world view. The Fejérváry Screenfold, pictured in Plate 4, is from what is now south central Mexico. Like the *mappae mundi*, its design is dominated by religious ideas (like the *mappae mundi* such maps were designed by the ruling and priestly classes), it represents time and space together, and the society from which the map stems is at its very centre.

One of the things which characterized the Columbian encounter between Europe and what was to become America was thus a meeting between very different ways of looking at the world. Indigenous peoples' knowledge of their geography was considerable. The 'meeting' was, of course, a highly unequal one but there is no doubt that native American geographical knowledge was a very important contribution to the colonizers' maps.

Yet the maps of colonizer and colonized were very different. They showed different things. There is some evidence, indeed, that the indigenous mappers, hired to help out the Spanish, persisted in representing their own societies on the maps as a 'conscious cartography of protest' (Harley, 1990, p. 121). But it was not to last. When Captain John Smith arrived in the north-east of what is now the United States of America, the first and most important thing to do was to name it (remember section 1.1.3?). He called it New England. It was a name which both erased the presence of the indigenous peoples and promoted the English cause against the competing claims of the Spanish, French and Dutch. He then set about mapping the place. As names with English references were added, indigenous place names were removed. Over the little-known interior, from where reports of indigenous nations had been received, was printed Smith's own portrait: 'Cartographers thus made visible the myth of an empty frontier. Supporting the ideology of conquest, maps became a tool to subdivide and bound the Indian territories. They portrayed an abstract geometrical space without people' (Harley, 1990, p. 136). As we saw in section 1.1, the struggle of people to put themselves back on the map is still going on.

1.2.2 The notion of the global

Notions of the earth and of the wider universe within which it is set have, then, changed and developed over time. Many early 'world maps' showed only a small portion of the globe even if set within a broader canvas, whether mythological, religious or astronomical. The Mesopotamian, Ebstorf and meso-American maps were all of this sort. Similar mixtures of local and global existed elsewhere too. Early Chinese maps were restricted in earthly terms to the provinces of China, around which was set a sea with a number of islands. Yet Chinese astronomy, even as early as the fifth century BC, was extremely advanced (Needham, 1959). In many societies, too, there were debates about whether other lands, as yet unknown, were inhabited. Early Buddhist scholars in India and China even hinted at human life elsewhere in the great expanse of the universe: 'How unreasonable it would be to suppose that besides the heaven and Earth which we can see there are no other heavens and no other earths!' (quoted in Berthon and Robinson, 1991, p. 39). For centuries, in China, in Africa, Australasia and the Americas, societies existed each with their own constructions of the world and its universe, each with their own ways of mapping them.

Our current mappings of the world are framed within the viewpoint of scientificity, and they can draw both on the accumulated knowledge of centuries and on the high-technology processes of recent years. And yet, even within the scientific framework there are still differences and debates about how the world can best be represented.

Activity 5   Turn now to Reading A by David Wright, entitled 'Maps with a message', which you will find at the end of this chapter. Do not worry about the details of different projections. Just concentrate on the main argument. In particular, try to relate these very modern debates to some of the issues so far raised in this chapter. For instance, what do you think of the points made about Pacific-centred maps? As you read, consider the following questions:

o   How might a Fijian feel about the first 'snag' mentioned?

o   Is it a problem of the map that the eastern hemisphere is on the left of the map and the western hemisphere on the right? Maybe it tells us something about who *named* the hemispheres 'western' and 'eastern' in the first place?!

Of course, the main point of this reading concerns the technical question of projections, of how to resolve the difficulty of representing the planet on a flat surface. Some kind of choice always has to be made. This is unavoidable. Moreover, it is not *only* a technical question. As Wright makes clear, different map projections reinforce different, and particular, views of the world.

Secondly, the reading shows how the question of how to centre the map is still a lively one. Even just by looking at a few national stamps he demonstrates this point. I identified five different centrings on the stamps alone.

However, thirdly and perhaps the most significant point of all, Wright concludes that 'No world map is "neutral", and none is totally "true"'. This does not, clearly, mean they are of no use. What is important is always to be aware of what the limitations are. This point applies to all kinds of maps, and all kinds of geographical representations, whether of the whole world or just a particular place. There is no 'view from nowhere'. There is always, inevitably, a particular perspective on things. The long historical story of our interpretation of the shape of the world is one which encompasses *both* actually increasing scientific knowledge *and* debates and contestations about how the world should be represented.

1.2.3   Monsters on the edge

Most maps of the world, quite understandably, concentrate on 'the known world'. Quite often, beyond a certain point, things become less detailed, knowledge is more hazy; and beyond that there is the unknown.

These regions of the less-known and the unknown have frequently been seen as threatening, and often this fear has been represented on maps. That earliest map we examined, of Babylon and Mesopotamia, showed beyond the waters of the encircling Bitter River a land where roamed legendary beasts. Ancient maps of China, so detailed in the geography of the known world, faded out around the margins into zones of 'allied barbarians' and, beyond that, into a zone of cultureless savagery. On the edges of Pliny's world (first century AD) were all kinds of creatures:

In the woods and groves beyond the north wind lived the Hyperboreans to whom death came only when, having had enough of life, they held a banquet, anointed their old age with luxury and leapt from a certain rock into the sea. There were the All-ears Islands whose inhabitants had very large ears covering the whole of their bodies, which were otherwise naked. In the middle of the African desert could be found the headless Blemmyae, whose mouth and eyes were on their chest. Along with hundreds more amazing peoples were animals such as the griffin, a wild, winged beast which mined gold; the tailed apes which had been known to play at draughts; the nereids, whose bodies bristled with hair even in the parts which were of human shape; the turtles of the Indian Ocean, which could be used as a roof for a house one way up and as a sailing boat the other.

(Berthon and Robinson, 1991, p. 29)

It was not always in the shape of monsters, but the new and the unknown had to be dealt with somehow. Sometimes, and in later centuries, people on the inner margins of the known world might be characterized as 'noble savages' or as simple people, perhaps living in an earthly paradise. Such views are uncomfortably close to, and still haunt, certain first world attitudes to other peoples.

Activity 6 Think back to the discussion, in section 1.1.4, of travel brochures and of views of the 'third world'. Do you think that sometimes they can resonate with such characterizations? (Think, for instance, of some of the brochures for 'exotic' tourist locations, and their depiction of friendly folk living an apparently simple life, far removed from the rush and tumble of normal existence in the industrialized West.)

Moreover, as the frontier of the less-known and the unknown is pushed back, so the tales of monsters, barbarians and simple folk themselves are moved. Many of the early monsters on European maps can be found in Asia and Africa. The Ebstorf world map, which I discussed earlier, did not only *focus on* Europe but *defined it* as Christian by clearly showing everything beyond as not-Christian. Beyond the Christian nations at the centre can be found the Jews and the Moslems and beyond them are Gog and Magog in Asia and the 'monstrous races' (as they were called) in Africa. Yet as Asia began to be explored the figures were relocated. The images which had once been used in an unknown Asia were later to be found populating the newly discovered continent of America.

And yet, before we smile, or adopt an attitude of condescension to all this, it would be well to examine how we construct even today our imaginative geographies. For what is going on here is a continuous process of definition and redefinition of people and places. As the edges of the known world are pushed back so we create and recreate our characterizations both of 'them' (other peoples) and of ourselves, and of 'our part of the world' and 'their part of the world'. That continuous process of the moulding of images is what is going on in such spheres as the travel information, news media and appeals for aid which were examined in section 1.1.4. And at the outer edges of our known world we still have our monsters and legendary beasts. Science fiction films of alien beings, whether terrifying strangers or lovable simple figures, perform the same kinds of function today as did the figures around the Ebstorf map in the thirteenth century. The way we imagine, and relate to, other peoples is a central issue of geography.

1.2.4 High-tech maps

Of course, nowadays we no longer make our maps from small intrepid boats feeling their way along a new coastline on a turbulent sea; nor do we have to rely on myths or hearsay for an idea of what lies beyond where we have actually been (or at least not as far as the globe itself is concerned). Nowadays we can make maps from photographs, we can even take pictures of the planet as a whole. Nowadays we can see the world as it really is. We no longer have to imagine.

Yet is that really so?

Among the sources of geographical data now available is a highly advanced and complex source known as 'Geographical Information Systems', or GIS. This is defined as a 'system for capturing, storing, checking, integrating, manipulating, analysing and displaying data which are spatially referenced to the Earth. This is normally considered to involve a spatially referenced computer database and appropriate applications of software' (HMSO, 1987; quoted in Cassetari and Parsons, 1993, p. 3).

The data can be displayed in a variety of forms: as maps, as photos, in tables, by postcode. It is, at least potentially, a hugely powerful system. And it can be used for many purposes from traffic planning to land-use disputes. Yet it must be remembered that this, too, like all other representations of the world, is a particular and partial view. For one thing, and inevitably, not everything is included, not even on a database. What *is* included will reflect the interests (in both senses of the word) of those who design the system. In fact, and as an illustration of this point, it is currently planned to put the indigenous people's alternative land use map of the Mosquitia on to GIS.

There have, moreover, been other reservations voiced about the neutrality of this way of looking at the world. Thus Roberts and Schein (1995) express concern about the relationship between this way of viewing the world and inequalities in social power. For, of course, only a few people and agencies, out of the population of the world as a whole, have access to this kind of technology. (The indigenous people of coastal Honduras are unlikely to be typical users. And the system on which their map is entered is not likely to be one of the powerful, global ones.) Given this, it is particularly important to explore the nature of the viewpoint this technology may represent. Roberts and Schein argue that 'Capturing the world within the computer is like buying or owning a piece, or potentially all, of the earth' (Roberts and Schein, 1995). This, they argue, is tied up with a particular aspect of the development of what we often think of as 'the scientific viewpoint': that it is distanced and detached; that the more distanced we are from what we are studying, the more 'objective', and scientific, is our research.

There are two questions which must be pursued here.

First, this distancing lends a feeling of power. Some of the data on systems like GIS come from satellites circling the earth. This way of collecting data, argue Roberts and Schein, makes the world seem passive and vulnerable beneath the all-seeing eye of the satellite. It is a way of seeing which resembles that of a voyeur, or a peeping-Tom. The satellite can see without being seen, into the daily lives of people miles below. And, indeed, a growing number of feminist philosophers and scientists have begun to have reservations about the characterization of science as an all-seeing distanced eye, and to explore other more participatory forms of knowledge. Such questions must remain especially important while so few have access, anyway, to this way of looking. In this age of 'globalization' we must continually ask, as Roberts does, 'The world is whose oyster?' (Roberts, 1994).

But there is also a second issue, related but perhaps even more fundamental. And that is whether, anyway, this process of 'taking your distance' does in fact produce a greater degree of objectivity. We have already mentioned this in relation to GIS, in the sense of some things necessarily being excluded while others are included. Let us now pursue it further by analysing one of the most 'distanced' maps of the world ever produced – a picture of the planet.

In November 1990 the *National Geographic* published a picture. It headlined it 'First-of-a-kind portrait from space', the work of Tom Van Sant and Lloyd Van Warren. This, then, is a different kind of high-tech map from GIS. The poster which was made of it was called 'A Clear Day'. It is reproduced in Plate 8. Here, surely, we have the world as it really is, brought to us in our own homes, by the power of satellite-imaging technology. Yet what kind of a portrait is it? Wood (1993) has produced a detailed examination of this question, and I follow it here.

Like all the other representations we have analysed in this chapter, from the map of Mesopotamia to the indigenous peoples' map of the Mosquitia, it had to be *produced*. There was a process of production. And such a process inevitably involves all kinds of social decisions and priorities and interests, just as did the maps of Mesopotamia and the Mosquitia. In the case of the Van Sant portrait just consider the following:

o   This is not the product of one photograph, but of dividing the earth's surface up into 35 million (yes, 35 million) pieces, recording each separately and then putting them together again.

o   Even these 'pixels' are not photographs, but scanner records which have then to be *turned into* photographic images.

o   The decision to use a scanner rather than other available technologies, the decision about what wavelength to use, the decision about the degree of resolution to be adopted – all these were decisions which had to be taken and, Wood demonstrates, all were influenced by a whole range of social forces, from military considerations to bureaucratic in-fighting.

o   The image produced from the scanner technology was then tinted. It was, effectively, painted (Van Sant is an artist, Van Warren a scientist at NASA's Jet Propulsion Laboratory). Colours had to be selected. Van Sant is cited as having selected colours which were 'realistic' (Wood, 1993, p. 55). But what does this mean? They are not the colours as recorded by the imaging technology. The planet at different distances, different angles and through different technologies, shows up in a range of colour-schemes. Van Sant in fact selected the colours we already have in our minds: the oceans are deep blue, the land varied with much green, there is grey-brown along the coasts where rivers flow out to sea, Antarctica is white. In other words, after all this technology, he produces the earth for us as we already imagine it.

All of these decisions reflect the fact that in the social production of *any* image some decisions just have to be made. Those decisions, however, will mean that one particular view is presented in preference to the range of other possibilities.

But the question of 'viewpoint' is even more clear in the issues of projection and centring. However far away the satellites go, they still have to take images of the earth from particular angles and/or present them in particular projections. The Van Sant map in the *National Geographic* uses the Robinson projection in which the equatorial regions appear smaller in relation to polar regions, which are enlarged. Greenland in Van Sant is 60 per cent enlarged in relation to the overall scale, and Africa fifteen per cent reduced in size. A necessary decision in the sense that a decision had to be taken, but a decision none the less. And what about the centring of the map? A decision had to be made here too.

Again, do any things strike you as odd about the picture? Well, for one thing, the whole globe is shown as being in daylight at the same time. Even if we were to accept the colours as realistic, this certainly is not. It is indeed physically impossible. It denies the fact that the earth turns on its axis – a not insignificant aspect of its reality. Or again, do you notice there are no clouds? The 35 million images were recorded at selected times. Or again, looking at the portrait, at what time of year would you think it was taken? In fact, 'Data from different times of year were acquired to ensure the best lighting and maximum vegetation' (Wood, 1993, p. 63). This, then, is a portrait not only without night and day but also without seasons. The images were collected across a three-year period.

Let us be clear what is being said here. As Wood argues, this procedure is not in some sense 'wrong'. The trouble comes only if the portrait is read as a 'true picture' of the world as it really is. Why, also, choose colours on the basis of 'realism' when, in order to get a good picture, you do the very *un*realistic thing of denying night and day, winter and summer? This is a *particular* view of the earth, a socially produced picture, and it could be no other.

Summary of section 1.2

o   No representation of the world can be 'neutral'. Each representation (each geographical imagination) necessarily has a particular perspective. We always need to be aware of this.

o   Maps of the world through the ages (like other forms of geographical representation) reflect the overall world views of the societies in which they were made.

o   The understanding of 'the shape of the world' has varied dramatically between societies and over time. Changes over time reflect both increasing scientific knowledge and debates about how the world should be represented.

o   All these debates continue, even within the currently dominant scientific world view.

o   One key aspect of the way in which we imagine/represent the world is how we deal with those parts which are less well-known. Images of 'others' may be important to our own sense of identity, but may also be problematical.

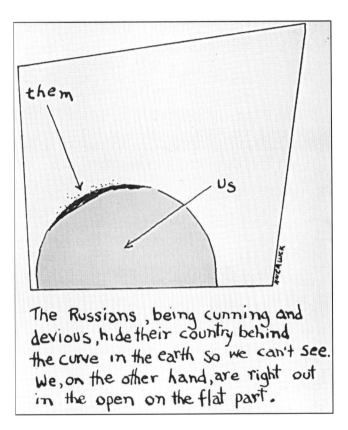

The Russians, being cunning and devious, hide their country behind the curve in the earth so we can't see. We, on the other hand, are right out in the open on the flat part.

1.3   Travellers' tales

1.3.1   Voyages of 'discovery'

There is a story told in China about Julius Caesar going to the theatre in a new coat. It was a coat woven from Chinese silk, and the audience was so impressed with it and curious about it that hardly anyone concentrated on the play. Even as long ago as that, there were the beginnings of contacts between the Chinese Empire and the Roman. The great Silk Road wound across deserts and mountain ranges from the western shores of the Pacific to the Mediterranean basin.

In 138 BC the Emperor of the Chinese Han Dynasty had sent an envoy, Chang Ch'ien, to journey westwards in search of potential allies. He made it as far as Bactria (today part of what we call Afghanistan) and was so taken with what he found that he stayed for a whole year. What in fact he had stumbled upon was an old outpost of Greek influence, for Bactria had even earlier been conquered and settled by Alexander the Great in the course of his long journey to India.

voyages of discovery

There are two points which strike me about these stories, and others of their kind. First, that travelling, trading and 'discovery' are age-old processes. In much of the West we tend to think of *voyages of discovery* in relation to the great period of European discoveries of the fifteenth century onwards. But it is an older and more diverse process than that. The Chinese must have felt they had 'discovered' Greek society when tales began to filter back. And that is the second point. That 'discovery' is not, or is only rarely, of empty continents and vast uninhabited lands. What voyagers of discovery most often discover is existing, complex societies. When Chang Ch'ien got to Bactria he 'was amazed to find "cities, mansions and houses as in China"' (Berthon and Robinson, 1991, pp. 40–1). When Vasco da Gama rounded the Cape of Good Hope into the great unknown of the Indian Ocean (in fact the Phoenicians had rounded it 2,000 years before!) he found that it 'was its own maritime world, buzzing with the traffic of Arab and Indian vessels, a long-established network of trade routes' (Berthon and Robinson, 1991, p. 75). And when Hernán Cortés hit Tenochtitlan (later to become Mexico City) 'some of our soldiers even asked whether the things they saw were not a dream' (Chronicle of Bernal Díaz, in Berthon and Robinson, 1991, p. 86).

Such discoveries had to be, somehow, incorporated into the world views of the discoverers, and often it caused that view to be altered. 'The shape of the world' was changed a little. Images of the new places and peoples had to be constructed and in this process the images which the 'discoverers' had of themselves, and of their own place in the world, were also often reworked. It is, in other words, an example of the process referred to in the concluding point of the Summary of section 1.2. (Re-read that point now, to refresh your memory.) The issue is how, both historically and today, we deal with what is new and what is different.

1.3.2 Alexander von Humboldt

For five years over the turn of the eighteenth century into the nineteenth, Alexander von Humboldt and Aimé Bonpland travelled and studied in South America and Mexico. The great number of volumes which Humboldt wrote upon his return were to have an enormous influence on the European public of the day, on its understanding of South America, and also on its understanding of the world as a whole. Mary Louise Pratt, in her analysis of Humboldt's writings, and their interpretation and effects, writes that 'Humboldt sought to reinvent popular imaginings of América, and through América, of the planet itself. ... Along with others of his time, he proposed to Europeans a new kind of planetary consciousness' (Pratt, 1992, pp. 119–20).

This was an age when the scientific endeavour as we know it was in its first flush and Humboldt was in many ways a product of (as well as a shaper of) that aspect of his age; he was an inveterate writer, note-taker, collector, documentor. But science in Europe was developing in a particular way: science was being cut off from sentiment, the 'objective' from the 'subjective', logic from feeling. Humboldt was opposed to this splitting and his writings rebel against it. This position framed his interpretation of, and his writings about, South America.

Perhaps above all, Humboldt's writings gave rise to an interpretation of South America as 'nature'. 'In the Old World', he wrote, 'nations and the distinctions of their civilization form the principal points in the picture; in the New World, man and his productions almost disappear amidst the stupendous display of wild and gigantic nature' (Humboldt, 1814, quoted in Pratt, 1992, p. 111). Not only was this nature, moreover; it was a glorious, powerful, dominant, vibrant Nature. Humboldt's descriptions sometimes are quite gripping: he exults, he is full of amazement. This, moreover, is a nature interpreted as having a harmony and a movement of its own; there is a feeling almost of something mystical, something occult, about it. In this it shares a perspective with the European Romantic movement of the time, and indeed that movement itself was powerfully influenced by proliferating stories of the 'new world'.

Yet, another side of the planetary consciousness to which Humboldt contributed was a clear, and particular, view of the-planet-as-a-whole. The tropical forests, the mountains and the stretching plains which Humboldt's writings made emblematic of the South American landscape were also set by him into a series of comparisons with other regions of the world. So the Venezuelan *llanos*, for instance, are compared to the heaths of northern Europe, the plains of Africa and the steppes of Central Asia (Pratt, 1992, p. 121). They were also by this means brought into the system of (European) thinking of the known world. As Pratt writes of natural history more generally: 'One by one the planet's life forms were to be drawn out of the tangled threads of their life surroundings and rewoven into European-based patterns of global unity and order' (Pratt, 1992, p. 31).

But remember: this was the beginning of the nineteenth century. Not only had there been great civilizations in South America (the Incas, for instance) but the Spanish had been there for 300 years. So to interpret it without seeing the people is quite a feat of the geographical imagination. Indeed, Humboldt did write to some extent about South American society, and even more of Mexican. He was indeed in many ways a progressive person, strongly opposed to slavery. And he frequently supported the interests of Latin

Americans against those of Imperial Spain (Fuentes, 1992, p. 251). Yet in some of his books the concentration on nature and the manner of its evocation enabled the presence of people to go unnoticed. In large part this was because of what the European reading public chose to draw from his writings: what they selected, what most thrilled them to read. But this in turn had effects. Humboldt's view of harmony extended to the relation between human beings and nature, and this could mean that the more wild and savage the nature so too the more wild and savage the people. And the

> For I have learned
> To look on nature, not as in the hour
> Of thoughtless youth, but hearing oftentimes
> The still, sad music of humanity,
> Not harsh nor grating, though of ample power
> To chasten and subdue.   And I have felt
> A presence that disturbs me with the joy
> Of elevated thoughts ; a sense sublime
> Of something far more deeply interfused,
> Whose dwelling is the light of setting suns,
> And the round ocean, and the living air,
> And the blue sky, and in the mind of man,
> A motion and a spirit, that impels
> All thinking things, all objects of all thought,
> And rolls through all things.   Therefore am I still
> A lover of the meadows and the woods,
> And mountains; and of all that we behold
> From this green earth; of all the mighty world
> Of eye and ear, both what they half-create,*
> And what perceive ; well pleased to recognize
> In nature and the language of the sense,
> The anchor of my purest thoughts, the nurse,
> The guide, the guardian of my heart, and soul
> Of all my moral being.

> * This line has a close resemblance to an admirable line of Young, the exact expression of which I cannot recollect.

An extract from William Wordsworth's *Lines Composed a Few Miles Above Tintern Abbey, On Revisiting the Banks of the Wye During a Tour, July 13, 1798,* an example of an English Romantic's view of nature dominance of nature over even this human presence reduced indigenous peoples' importance still more. Here, it seemed, at the dawn of the industrial revolution was a whole continent whose history – thought of like this – was yet to begin. It was waiting for development. Its history would start, or so the imagination might run, through European intervention. On this scenario, Humboldt's writings may have been a contribution to the formation of the geographical imagination of Europeans at that time, and in such a way that South America was imagined – was placed in the world – as awaiting European-led development. That kind of geographical imagination can, of course, help legitimize imperialistic pretensions.

1.3.3   *The Old Patagonian Express*

Travel writing continues to this day to be a powerful way in which we form our geographical imaginations.

Activity 7   Turn now to the extracts from Paul Theroux's *The Old Patagonian Express: By Train Through the Americas* in Reading B at the end of this chapter. Paul Theroux is a very well-known and popular writer, and these readings cannot do justice to the range of his work. But these extracts from one of his most famous books provide an illuminating contrast with the writings of Humboldt. As you read, try to think about these contrasts. In particular, concentrate on:

o   the writer's attitude to the natural world;

o   his relation to Latin American society (here Theroux is writing of Mexico);

o   the way in which he expects his readers to think of *themselves*.

Perhaps the clearest contrast with Alexander von Humboldt is in the lack of wonderment which Paul Theroux conveys. Although these extracts are more about the social than the natural world, this lack of awe is even evident in the treatment of nature. The desert is merely 'rough', 'stony' and lacking in trees. Moreover, while Humboldt had to decide what he thought were the typical elements of the South American landscape (plains, mountains and forests), Theroux already knows to associate 'Mexico' and 'cactus'. As the breaking dawn gradually clarifies the view, the cactus has an 'emblematic quality'. At this point in the book Theroux has only been in Mexico a short time. One gets the feeling that the identification of Mexico with cacti is something he packed in his suitcase in Boston and brought with him! And indeed, as any of us travel today, two hundred years after Humboldt, it is hard *not* to have some pre-packed 'typical' images which we may dutifully write home about or capture with our cameras. The pre-formed geographical imagination is very powerful.

What Theroux does do in a lot more detail than Humboldt, however, is write about people. One cannot possibly interpret Theroux as underplaying the human presence. The nearly two centuries between the two writers also influence, moreover, the way in which that presence can be interpreted. This is no longer a land which can plausibly be interpreted as simply waiting for development, and particularly not development through the agency of first world countries. There has already been a long history of intervention and informal imperialism.

In that context, two things are particularly striking about the way Theroux writes. First, he assumes a position of absolute authority. He does not seem to doubt for a minute his right to pass the sweeping judgements he records. He generalizes with an easy confidence about 'Mexicans' and 'Mexico'. Second, he sees much of Mexican life, in these passages, in terms of poverty and degradation. The dogs are often lame, the people 'beaten'. This is the era of greater consciousness of poverty and hardship in other parts of the world.

In pointing to these perspectives on Mexican society Theroux is taking us way beyond some other views we might come across: views which paint Mexico entirely in the colours of the Aztec and Mayan civilizations of the past, maybe; or tourist brochures which concentrate on pyramids, with an occasional day off from culture to lounge on a palm-fringed Caribbean coast; or perspectives which collapse the variety and complexity of this country into a fun-packed Acapulco. Theroux's writing here is quite distinct from these approaches, and arguably also presents a 'richer' view, in which the reader is invited to be more than a consumer of pyramids and beaches.

And that, of course, is part of the attraction of Theroux's writing. He is saying to us, his readers, "I am not – and you are not either, are you? – just one of those unthinking mass tourists". *We* see beyond all that. The appeal is that this is realistic writing (warts and all), not for the mere tourist but for the experienced *traveller*. Theroux pays us the compliment of assuming we do not need telling about the basics of this place. As he writes of 'that curious Mexican mixture of sparkle and decay, blue sky and bedragglement', he is inviting us to nod wisely (we already know, don't we, or are happy to acquiesce in pretending to know) that that mixture is indeed precisely Mexican. Not only is he constructing a Mexico for us, but he is also constructing us, the readers. And he is, thereby, also constructing the relationship *between* Mexico and us, the knowing travellers.

And here Theroux's tone is important; the air of first world superiority which he can fall into may all too easily mirror the relative economic and cultural positions in the world of the United States, from where he comes, and Mexico. We may, as we read the passages, feel willing to share in the author's authority and his easy disparagement of so much of what he sees. Or we may question this treatment of Mexico and seek out others. Or we may, perhaps particularly if we are women, feel that Paul Theroux's experience could not be ours anyway; feel that this is not just a particular first world view but also a male view, which can refer to Mexican women as 'those willing girls'. (Indeed, it is perhaps worth pondering just how much of our understanding of the world is relayed to us by the male voice choir of explorers, travellers, reporters, and so on. There is now a burgeoning literature on women travellers and the way in which they do often write their travellers' tales rather differently.) Perhaps, in his characterization of the prostitution as 'comic and rather pleasant', Theroux is in fact playing to the same images of 'third world' women as does the increasingly 'mass' industry of sex tourism.

Even in the earliest days, 'discovery' was never simply 'discovery'. It was always also necessarily a process of interpretation and presentation, of choice of view. And this 'choice of view' was important. Whether it be tales of barbarians, idyllic images of 'happy, simple people', helpless famine victims with hands outstretched for aid, or people with lives and views of their own, this aspect of our imaginary geography strongly conditions our relations with others. And today, travellers' tales continue that process, constantly filling out our geographical imaginations and, thereby, interpreting our own place in the world we imagine.

Summary of section 1.3

o Voyages of 'discovery' usually involve 'discovery' of other societies, and this process provokes changes in our geographical imaginations, in particular about our own and others' identities.

o Travel writing through the ages continues this process, and reflects the understandings of the world, and their positions in it, of both writers and readers.

1.4   Conclusion

The way we understand the geographical world, and the way in which we *represent* it, to ourselves and to others, is what is called our 'geographical imagination'. It is through this geographical imagination that people and societies understand their place in the world, and the place, too, of other people and other societies. Such world views vary between societies and through history. They may also be contested. They are social products which reflect a balance of power. Maps are just one means of representation of world views, and all maps necessarily present a particular understanding of the world. But many other things too – from tourist brochures to the news to travel programmes on the television – contribute to the formation of our geographical imaginations. Being able to interpret these sources is important, because the nature of geographical imaginations – our views of the shape of the world – can be of fundamental importance to how we act within it.

References

BERTHON, S. and ROBINSON, A. (1991) *The Shape of the World: the Mapping and Discovery of the Earth*, London, George Philip.

CASSETARI, S. and PARSONS, E. (1993) 'What is GIS?', mimeo for seminar, available from GIS Short Course Administrator, School of Geography, Penrhyn Road, Kingston, Surrey KT1 2EE, UK.

FUENTES, C. (1992) *El Espejo Enterrado*, Mexico, Fondo de Cultura Económica.

HARLEY, J.B. (1990) *Maps and the Columbian Encounter*, Milwaukee, WI, University of Wisconsin, The Golda Meir Library.

HMSO (DEPARTMENT OF THE ENVIRONMENT) (1987) *Handling Geographic Information: Report to the Secretary of State for the Environment of the Committee of Inquiry into the Handling of Geographic Information* (The Chorley Report; chairman, Lord R. Chorley), London, HMSO.

HUMBOLDT, A., VON (1814) *Personal Narrative of Travels to the Equinoctal Regions of the New Continent*, translated by H.M. Williams, London, Longman *et al.*, 1822.

NEEDHAM, J. (1959) *Science and Civilization in China*, Cambridge, Cambridge University Press.

PRATT, M.L. (1992) *Imperial Eyes: Travel Writing and Transculturation*, London, Routledge.

PTOLEMY, C. (1991) *The Geography*, New York, Dover Publications.

ROBERTS, S.M. (1994) 'The world is whose oyster?', mimeo, available from the author, Department of Geography, University of Kentucky, Lexington, KY 40506-0027, USA.

ROBERTS, S.M. and SCHEIN, R.H. (1995) 'Earth shattering: global imagery and GIS', in Pickles, J. (ed.) *Ground Truth: the Social Implications of Geographic Information Systems*, New York, The Guilford Press.

THEROUX, P. (1980) *The Old Patagonian Express: By Train Through the Americas*, Harmondsworth, Penguin.

WOOD, D. (1993) *The Power of Maps*, London, Routledge.

WRIGHT, D.R. (1993) 'Maps with a message', *Geographical*, Vol. LXV, No. 1, pp. 37–41.

[...]

No map on flat paper can be totally 'true'. The problem comes when people forget this fact. Perhaps every world map should carry a 'geographical health warning'.

The basic problem can be summarized as the **'triangle with three right angles'** phenomenon (Figure A.1). Everyone knows that such a triangle is impossible – yet the 0 and 90⁰E lines of longitude obviously make a right-angle at the North Pole. Both these lines also cross the Equator at right-angles. The triangle has angles totalling 270 degrees instead of 180. No flat map can reproduce this adequately – yet these lines only enclose one-eighth of the area of the globe. To put the whole globe on flat paper increases the problem by at least eight times.

One approach to mapping the world is to fit a cylinder of paper round the globe (Figure A.2). There is no problem with the Equator when the cylinder is 'unwrapped', but for the rest of the globe there are major problems.

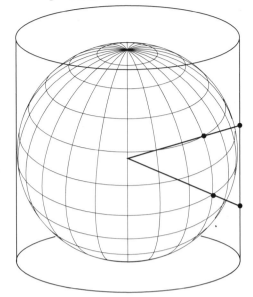

Figure A.2 *Cylindrical projection (Source: Kingfisher Pocket Atlas, J. & D. Wright, p. 22)*

these types of maps are in use, as the examples will show. They are all 'cylindrical' map projections.

The **Mercator projection** is the best-known of the 'stretch' maps. Land shapes are excellent – but Greenland, Canada and Russia appear far bigger than they really are. Even 'little' Britain is 'Great' in size, by comparison with the tropical lands.

It is no accident that Canada chose to use a Mercator map in 1898 (Figure A.3). It was the first time a world map had ever appeared on a stamp, and it became very well known. Although it was

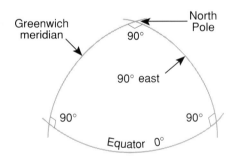

Figure A.1 *Triangle with three right angles*

The three basic approaches to the problem of 'unwrapping' the globe onto flat paper can be described as 'stretch', 'squash' or 'snip'. An 'equal-stretch' map can keep **shapes** correct, but harms the scale; a 'squash' map can keep **scale** correct, but harms the shapes. A compromise ('strash'? or 'squetch'?) can offer less extreme distortion of scale and shape, but it is not accurate in either respect.

Finally, a policy of 'snipping' can keep size and scale almost correct by putting the distortions into the cuts. These cuts are normally made in the oceans. All

Figure A.3 *The world's first map-stamp in 1898 used the Mercator projection to reinforce its message*

a Christmas stamp, the message was not 'Peace on earth'. The choice of projection emphasized the chosen message: 'We hold a vaster empire than has been'.

Mercator maps were the standard classroom wall-map for many years, and this misleading image of the world has entered deeply into general consciousness. Many Europeans still have an exaggerated view of the size of the northern continents, and are unaware of the size of Africa.

Nevertheless, the Mercator map is still the best map for **navigators**, because a constant bearing appears as a straight line. So Mercator has a bright future – not a bad achievement for a 420-year-old map projection. But it does not deserve a prominent place in schools, and certainly not on the walls of geography classrooms or lecture-rooms. (If it's still there, take it down!)

The unfair treatment of the tropics on the Mercator map was a major reason for the publication of the **Peters Projection** in 1973 (Figure A.4). But the Peters

Projection, which has been promoted with such enthusiasm as an antidote to the errors of Mercator, is equally misleading in some ways. On this map, the errors are in the shapes. In reality, Africa is as 'wide' (east–west) as it is long (north–south) – yet people brought up on the Peters map tend to assume that Africa is twice as long as it is wide. If you feel that a square country should appear as an oblong, this is fine – but for the rest of us the Peters map certainly needs a bold 'geographical health warning'.

Nevertheless, Peters has one huge virtue – it is an **'equal-area' map**. Any one area of the earth is at the same scale as any other area. So there is no danger of ignoring any part of the world simply because it appears to be very small.

It can be argued that Peters has achieved three remarkable feats:

1 He has made people interested in map projections, and in the distortion of maps.
2 He has persuaded the general public that an equal-area projection is vital.

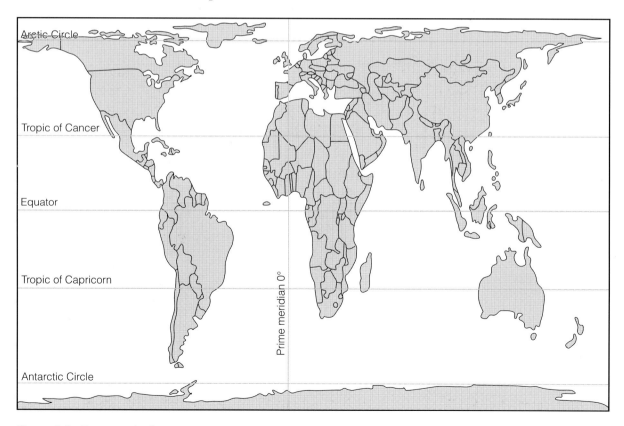

Figure A.4 *Peters projection*

3   He has convinced many people that his projection is the best – but the general public has not realized that there are other equal-area projections to choose from.

No-one will complain about the first of these achievements, and the second is important: we are all liable to draw the wrong conclusions from a map that is not equal-area. It is the third point that is the controversial one. Much of the confusion in discussing Peters' map is caused by not distinguishing between his three different achievements.

There are actually several other equal-area map projections which do not have the huge distortions of Peters. Any good atlas will name the map projection it uses. For example, '**Hammer**' is one useful equal-area projection – see *Philips' Modern School Atlas*. It has been said that Mr Hammer 'hammered' north-east Asia to fit it into his map! All equal-area projections inevitably have some errors of shape […]

The 'strash/squetch' group of map projections represents a compromise between the extreme size distortions of Mercator and the extreme shape distortions of some equal-area projections such as Peters. The Reverend James **Gall**, a Victorian clergyman, produced a map projection (Figure A.5) that has reasonable shapes and much less distortion of size than Mercator. Surprisingly, the projection by this long-dead clergyman is the chosen map for launching the [UK] Geography National Curriculum in schools. Today's A-level students escaped just in time – but it can be confidently predicted that future citizens will have a 'Gall-shaped' world deeply embedded in their sub-conscious.

The weakness of Gall is that it is not equal-area: Canada, Greenland and the CIS are too big. There is a real danger here, because the distortions are not as obvious as they are on the Mercator map. The National Curriculum document adds to the problem by stating that the map is equal-area when it isn't.

Unfortunately there is no way that a round world can be portrayed both with accurate size and accurate shape. Apart from warnings, are there any solutions to this problem? The best and simplest

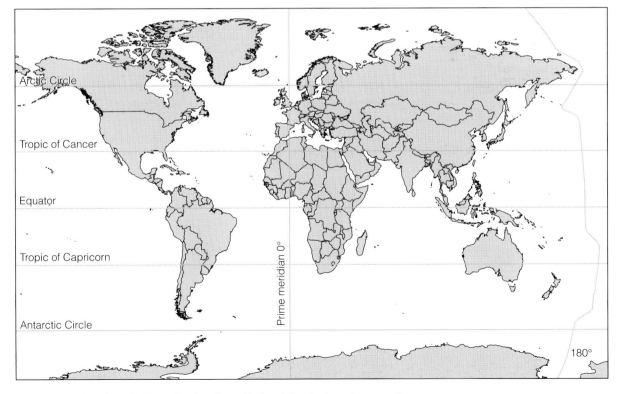

Figure A.5   *Modified Gall's projection (from National Curriculum document)*

answer is to have a globe in every classroom, in every lecture room, and in as many homes as possible. But we still need world maps. Arguably the next-best solution to the round world/flat map problem is to cut the map in several places. Every map does this at the edges, so the concept is already present. All that is needed are some extra cuts. Most of the distortions can be absorbed into the cuts instead of misleading us in the map itself. And the maps can be 'equal-area' too.

One good example is **Mollweide's interrupted equal-area** (or **homolographic**) projection. The Australian stamp has one 'snip' less than the UN stamp: the comparison (Figures A.6 and A.7) shows the alternatives. There is no real problem in the southern hemisphere, because there are three oceans. But in the northern hemisphere, one either has a stretched and distorted effect in Eastern Asia, or an awkward cut in the middle of Siberia. Neither solution is perfect – but both maps are far more accurate in size and

shape than any of the 'uncut' maps. The cuts are such obvious imperfections that they cause no problems in understanding.

There is another form of distortion that all the maps so far discussed usually share: they are usually centred on Europe and Africa, and all leave the Pacific at the edge of the world. Sometimes it is helpful to see an American-centred map (such as the 1898 Canada stamp). More distinctive is a **Pacific-centred** map – though they are hard to find. The North Korean stamp has a Pacific-centred Hammer projection. A stamp from Fiji shows a real rarity: a Pacific-centred interrupted map (Figures A.8 and A.9).

However, Pacific-centred maps have two major snags. All the other maps can 'lose' distortions in the huge Pacific ocean; but a Pacific-centred map has to distort the major land-masses very seriously. Secondly, the western hemisphere is printed on the right (east?) and the eastern hemisphere is on the left (west?) – a sure way to cause

Figures A.6 and A.7 'Cut' maps are less misleading than most projections – but where do you put the cuts? The Australian stamp (Figure A.6) and the United Nations one (Figure A.7) show two different ways of dividing the globe, one with an extra snip

Figure A.8 The stamp from North Korea is a Pacific-centred Hammer projection

Figure A.9 The Fijian stamp is a rarity: a Pacific-centred interrupted map

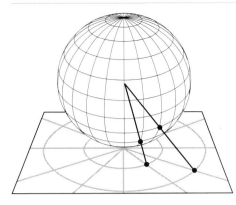

Figure A.10 *Polar zenithal projection* (Source: *Kingfisher Pocket Atlas*, J. & D. Wright, p. 23)

confusion. Nevertheless, the maps are a useful way of challenging our assumptions.

Another approach to world mapping is to choose a specific point as the centre (**zenith**) and to use a **zenithal** (or **azimuthal**) map projection (Figure A.10). One useful map, even if rather 'self-centred' is a map centred on one's own part of the world. In 1948, post-war Britain hosted the Olympic Games. The map-stamp (Figure A.11) shows Britain at the centre of the world. There is a remarkably three-dimensional effect, predating satellite pictures by many years. Its weakness is that it can only show half the world.

Figure A.11 *Britain was shown at the centre of the world to commemorate the 1948 Olympics*

To get the whole world shown on a zenithal projection, one can show two sides of the globe: the 'western' and 'eastern' hemispheres. Thus the King of Great Britain was pleased to appear in the centre of the world in a stamp issued in 1949! (Figure A.12). The stamp from

Figure A.12 *1949's King-centred stamp*

Cuba shows the world centred on Cuba and on the antipodes of Cuba (Figure A.13).

Any point on the globe can be chosen as the centre of a zenithal map. Even Antarctic-centred maps exist, centred on the South Pole. On the stamp from Australia shown in Figure A.14, the southern parts of Australia and South America can be seen, and the extreme south of Africa just appears by the 'N' of 'AUSTRALIAN' – but most of the world's land is missing.

Figure A.13 *This stamp shows a world centred on Cuba*

Figure A.14 *An Australian Antarctic-centred zenithal map*

Figure A.15 *This zenithal map is centred on the North Pole and encircled by the UN flag*

Much better known is a zenithal map centred on the North Pole. It is on the UN flag, as shown on the stamp from the UK in Figure A.15. This is a very effective map for the northern hemisphere, but it tends to marginalize the southern hemisphere, and it distorts Australia badly. If Antarctica were to appear, it would be a circle around the edge of the map. Nevertheless, great ingenuity has been used in plotting parts of the world that cannot be seen when looking at the North Pole on a globe. The map loses the 3-D effect seen on the 1948 British stamp, but gains in the percentage of the world shown.

A very rare but effective alternative is an **interrupted polar zenithal** map. The southern continents appear as the points of a star and the distortions are much less serious (Figure A.16).

Figure A.16 *Interrupted polar zenithal map*

Perhaps the last word should be left to a map-stamp which makes no attempt at perfect accuracy, but which has a powerful message. The USA has recently issued a stamp with an 'interrupted' map projection which uses only one cut. It conveys the most important geographical message of all (Figure A.17).

Conclusion: no world map is 'neutral', and none is totally 'true'. Most world maps have some good qualities, but all have limitations. It is important to understand what these limitations are.

Source: Wright, 1993, pp. 37–41

Figure A.17 *The most important map-message of all? This one needed only one cut and makes no attempt at geographical accuracy*

Reading B: *Paul Theroux, extracts from* The Old Patagonian Express: By Train Through the Americas

[...] I pushed up the shade and saw the sun rising behind a green tree. It was a solitary tree, and the climbing sun gave it an emblematic quality in the stony landscape; it was a pale perpendicular, studded with fruit like hand grenades, but as I watched it, it thickened and grew less tree-like and finally stiffened into a cactus.

There were more cactuses, some like burnt-out torches and others the more familiar candelabras. There were no trees. The sun, so early in the morning, was bright and gave a blueness to the hills which twisted off into the distance, and a glitter to the stiletto spikes on the cacti. The long morning shadows lay as still and dark as lakes and patterned the rough ground with straight margins. I wondered whether it was cold outside until I saw a man – the only human in that desert – in a donkey cart, rumbling over a road that might well have been a creek-bed. The man was dressed warmly, his sombrero jammed over his ears, a maroon scarf wrapped around his face, and a wadded jacket of brilliantly coloured rags.

It was still early. As the sun moved higher in the sky, the day became warmer and woke the smells, until that curious Mexican mixture of sparkle and decay, blue sky and bedragglement, asserted itself. In the bright air was the dismal town of Bocas. Here were four green trees, and a church on a steep hill, its whitewash reddened by dust, and cactuses so large cows were tethered to their spiky trunks. But most of the town was mimicry: the church was a house, the houses were sheds, most trees were cactuses, and without topsoil the crops – red peppers and corn – were skeletal. Some children in torn clothes skipped over to look at the train, and then, hearing the honk of a horn, ran to the sandy road to see a heavily-laden Coca-Cola truck – up to its axles in sand – straining towards the town's one store.

Mexicans habitually site the town dump along the railway tracks. The detritus of the very poor is unimaginably vile, and though it smoulders it is far too loathsome to catch fire. In the Bocas dump, which was part of Bocas station, two dogs yanked at one heap of garbage, two pigs at another. These animals went on rooting – keeping their distance – and I noticed that both dogs were lame, and one pig's ear was missing. The mutilated animals were appropriate to the mutilated town, the ragged children, the tumbledown sheds. The Coca-Cola truck had parked. Now the children were watching a man dragging a frantic pig across the tracks. The pig's hind legs were roped, and the man yanked the screaming creature backwards.

I do not consider myself to be an animal-lover, but it is a long way from disliking them to maiming and torturing them. And I came to see a resemblance between the condition of domestic animals and the condition of the people who mistreated them. It was the same contempt, and the whipped dog and the woman carrying wood had the same fearful eyes. And it was these beaten people who beat their animals.

[...]

I had arrived in Veracruz at seven in the morning, found a hotel in the pretty Plaza Constitucion and gone for a walk. I had absolutely nothing to do: I did not know a soul in Veracruz, and the train to the Guatemalan border was not leaving for two days. Still, this did not seem a bad place. There are few tourist attractions in Veracruz; there is an old fort and, about two miles south, a beach. The guidebooks are circumspect about describing this fairly ugly city: one calls it 'exuberant', another 'picturesque'. It is a faded seaport, with slums and tacky modernity crowding the quaintly ruined buildings at its heart. Unlike any other Mexican city, it has pavement cafés, where forlorn children beg and marimba players complete the damage to your eardrums that was started on the descent from the heights of Orizaba. Mexicans treat stray children the way other people treat stray cats (Mexicans treat stray cats like vermin), taking them on their laps and buying them ice cream, all the while shouting to be heard over the noise of the marimbas.

[...]

To flatter myself that I had something important to do in Veracruz I made a list of provisions that I intended to buy for my trip to Guatemala. Then I remembered I had no ticket. I went immediately to the railway station.

'I cannot sell you a ticket today,' said the man at the window.

'When can I buy one?'

'When are you leaving?'

'Thursday.'

'Fine. I can sell you one Thursday.'

'Why can't I buy one today?'

'It is not done.'

'What if there are no seats on Thursday?'

He laughed. 'On *that* train there are always seats.'

That was the day I met the taxi driver who said he had a whore for me who was 'not pretty at all'. I said I was not interested, but what else was there to do in Veracruz? He said I should go to the Castle. I said I had been to the Castle. Go for a walk around the city, he said: lovely churches, good restaurants, bars full of prostitutes. I shook my head. 'Too bad you were not here a few days ago,' he said. 'The carnival was fantastic.'

'Maybe I'll go swimming,' I said.

[...]

I had planned to get to bed early in order to be up at dawn to buy my ticket to Tapachula. It was when I switched the light off that I heard the music; darkness gave the sounds clarity, and it was too vibrant to be coming from a radio. It was a strong, full-throated brass band:

Land of Hope and Glory, Mother of the Free,

How shall we extol thee, who are born of thee?

'Pomp and Circumstance'? In Veracruz? At eleven o'clock at night?

Wider still and wider shall thy bounds be set;

God who made thee mighty, make thee mightier yet.

I dressed and went downstairs.

In the centre of the Plaza, near the four fountains, was the Mexican Navy Band, in white uniforms, giving Elgar the full treatment. Lights twinkled in the boughs of the laburnum trees, and there were floodlights, too – pink ones – playing on the balconies and the palms. A sizeable crowd had gathered to listen – children played near the fountain, people walked their dogs, lovers held hands. The night was cool and balmy, the crowd good-humoured and attentive. I think it was one of the prettiest sights I have ever seen; the Mexicans had the handsome thoughtful look, the serenity that comes of listening closely to lovely music. It was late, a soft wind moved through the trees, and the tropical harshness that had seemed to me constant in Veracruz was gone; these were gentle people, this was an attractive place.

The song ended. There was clapping. The band began playing 'The Washington Post March', and I strolled around the perimeter of the plaza. There was a slight hazard in this. Because the carnival had just ended, Veracruz was full of idle prostitutes, and as I strolled I realized that most of them had not come here to the plaza to listen to the band –

in fact, the greater part of the audience was composed of dark-eyed girls in slit skirts and low-cut dresses who, as I passed them, called out, 'Let's go to my house', or fell into step with me and murmured, 'Fuck?' This struck me as comic and rather pleasant – the military dignity of the march music, the pink light on the lush trees and balconies of the plaza, and the whispered invitations of those willing girls.

Source: Theroux, 1980, pp. 61–3, 77, 79, 81–2

Local worlds

by Richard Meegan

Chapter 2

2.1 Global connections and local worlds

2.1.1 Global connections

The previous chapter began with the local world of Mosquitia and the struggles over the understanding of that world by the people currently inhabiting it. Central to these struggles was cartography – the 'mapping out' of two conflicting views of the geography of that 'local world'. I hope it became clear from the discussion that the geography in question was not shaped solely by local factors but was also conditioned by the local world's historical connections with outside 'worlds' (most notably, for example, in the guise of the colonial slave traders who forcibly transported the Garífunas from Africa to St Vincent, the stopping-off point for the subsequent migration to mainland Honduras). In this chapter I want to develop this idea of the local connection with the global by looking at the 'local world' in which I currently live and work, Liverpool.

Figure 2.1 is a shameless variant of what Doreen Massey in the previous chapter referred to as the rule of ethnocentricity – putting your own place, in this case Liverpool, in the centre of the map. This, however, is a deliberate move on my part to make the point that there is some historical justification for locating Liverpool in the centre of the map. The city did have a central role to play in one particular phase of world economic development – the phase of European mercantile expansion across the globe during the sixteenth, seventeenth and eighteenth centuries. The social relations around which this colonial world-economy was structured helped to shape Liverpool's very particular 'local world' at that time.

global connections

A number of other places have also been picked out on the map as examples of a range of historical *global connections*. In Africa, there are the old slave trading towns of Bonny and Old Calabar on the former Slave Coast of West

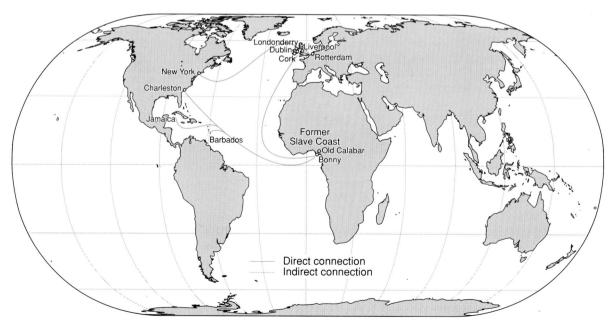

Figure 2.1   Global connections: Liverpool and other 'local worlds'

Africa. There are the connections with the West Indies, represented on the map by Barbados and Jamaica, and those with Charleston and New York in the USA. Londonderry, Cork and Dublin in Ireland are there to represent links made through flows of migration while Rotterdam appears chiefly as representative of new relationships being forged in Europe.

Places can be viewed as being linked in an evolving web of *interconnections*. In this web, at different points in time, some connections between places will be more direct, and the ties of mutual dependency stronger, than are others. Looking back at Figure 2.1, you will see how the connection between Liverpool and Rotterdam has been differentiated from the others shown on the map. The link is distinguished as being one of indirect connection in contrast to the historically more direct links joining the other places on the map to Liverpool.

interconnection

2.1.2   Local worlds and social relations

It is worth stopping at this point to think about what is meant by the term 'local world'. You have been presented with a map on which a number of places have been located (Liverpool, New York, Charleston, Rotterdam, etc.), and told that these are related in some way. But before moving on we need to be clear about what we mean by 'place', by 'local world' and by 'related'.

Places and their local worlds refer to a part of social space in which people live, work and socialize, and the interaction over time of these activities gives places their distinctiveness. To understand a place and how it has changed over time it is necessary to understand the evolving interplay between different *social relations* (in work, in social life outside work, and in political activity) in that place. Social relations make places, make local worlds. But how does this help one to understand the interrelationship between places? Well, the point to grasp is that social relations within places are also related to those operating across and between them. The social relations that constitute a place – a place that almost by definition is unique – are not all confined to that place.

social relations

To understand a place and how it has changed over time, then, it is also necessary to understand that not all the social relations helping to shape that place are confined to it. Some stretch beyond it. One way of looking at this relationship is to envisage social relations – economic, political and cultural – as being stretched across space, some remaining within the boundaries of a place and others stretching beyond them. It is this stretching of social relations across space that connects places and the people who live in them with other places and other people. This complex geography of social relations is dynamic; it is constantly developing as social relations ebb and flow and new relations are constructed. And it is the combination over time of local and wider, external social relations that gives places their distinctiveness.

Moreover, given that places are *constructed* through social relationships, the question of how we define and *represent* places to ourselves and others is always present. Do individuals and groups define themselves in relation to the places in which they live? Do they *identify* with them? Individuals or groups in the same place may identify very differently with it and may represent it very differently both to themselves and to outsiders. Similarly, individuals and groups living outside particular places may have

construction of place
representation of place
identification with place

representations of those places which differ greatly from the representations of people who live in them. And, just as the geography of social relations is constantly changing, so too are people's identifications with, and representations of, the places that are being reconstituted within this evolving geography.

Activity 1 Before reading on, reflect for a moment on a place that you know well. What links has it had with other places? What links does it have now? How have these connections affected it.

Think also about the social relationships that, for you, define that place: family relations, personal relations with other local people, work relations and the cross-cutting relations of race, ethnicity and gender that combine to 'place' you.

Try to distinguish between relations that are constructed and operate at the local level and those that are 'stretched' across space to other places and consider how these different relations interact. Some of your family, for example, may live locally while others are spread across the world. You may work for a local firm that is part of an overseas-owned transnational corporation with decision-taking powers located elsewhere and with your local firm's performance constantly being compared with that of the corporation's other activities dotted around the world. Think about your political affiliations and how these are expressed in different political arenas: local government, national parliament, and, if appropriate, European Parliament. Think about the different, often overlapping, relations in which your local ward councillor, your constituency MP, and your MEP are involved.

In the next section I want to describe some aspects of the different connections between Liverpool and the other places shown on Figure 2.1. Then, section 2.3 will go on to discuss some of the ways in which these connections have helped to constitute and reconstitute different aspects of the local worlds that are Liverpool. I shall also try to show that representations of places, of Liverpool in this case, are themselves rooted in the connections between places. Again using Liverpool as an example, the emphasis in the final section will be on the need to understand changing local worlds in the context of uneven geographical development. The relative decline of the city of Liverpool is related to its changing role in the world economy and its changing global connections. An attempt will be made to argue that these changed circumstances have raised anew issues of the identity and representation of places.

It must be emphasized that Liverpool is being used to illustrate general arguments on the construction, identification and representation of places. It should not be seen as being some kind of special case. It is unique and special for the people who live in it, but so too are other places and these could just as easily have been used to illustrate the arguments. So try to focus on the arguments being made rather than on the local detail and think about similarities to and differences from places with which you are more familiar.

Plate 1 Babylonian clay tablet map. By courtesy of the British Museum

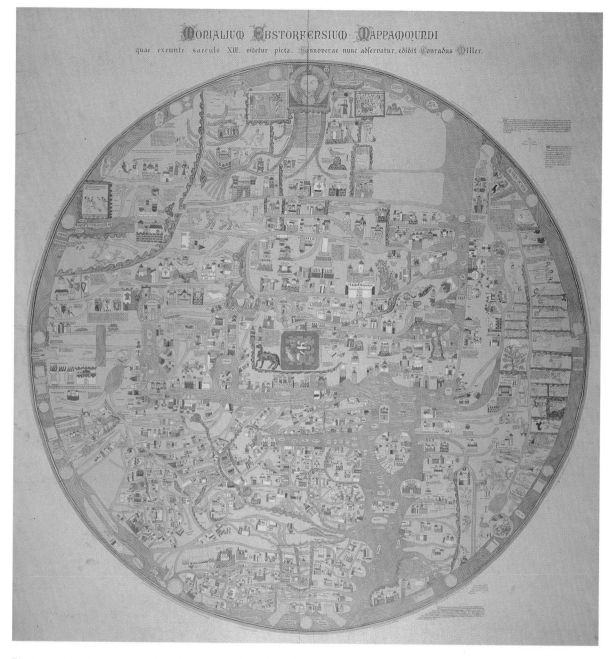

Plate 2 *The Ebstorf Map, circa 1240. Size of original: 3.56 x 3.58 m. By courtesy of the William L. Clements Library, University of Michigan*

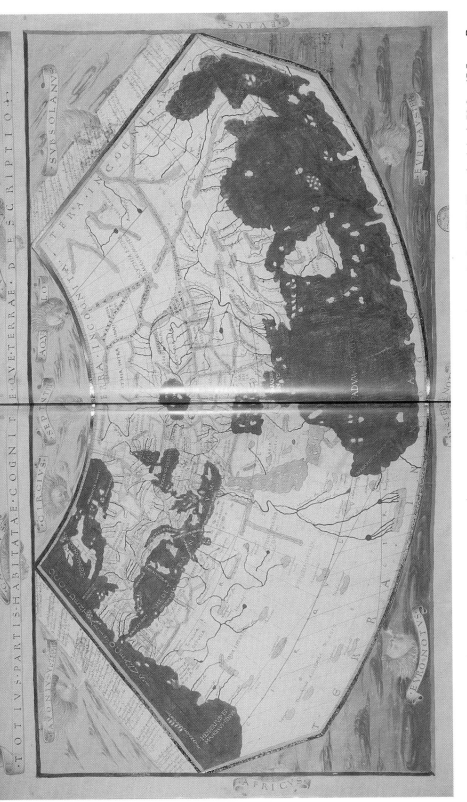

Plate 3 Claudius Ptolemy, world map from the Latin manuscript of the Geographia, Codex Vaticanus Latinus 277. Size of original: 59.3 × 45.5 cm. By courtesy of the American Geographical Society Collection, University of Wisconsin-Milwaukee Library

Plate 4 Page one from the Codex Fejérváry Mayer, pre-Columbian, Mixteca-Puebla culture. Size of original: 17.5 x 17.5 cm. By courtesy of the Board of Trustees of the National Museums and Galleries on Merseyside

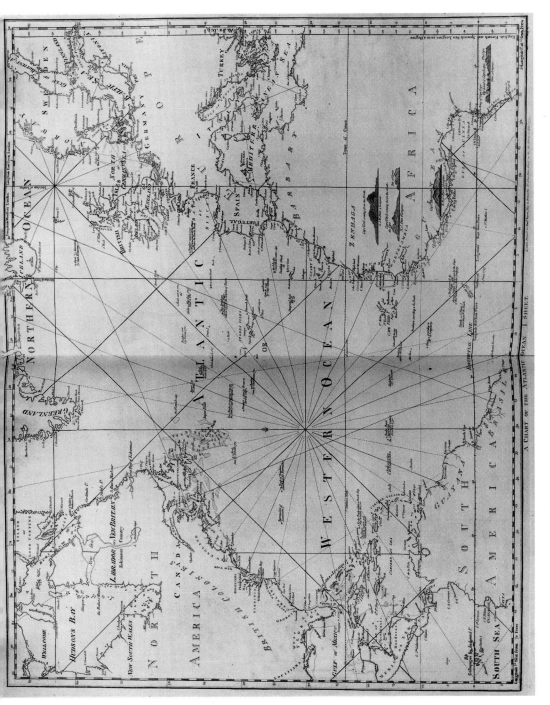

Plate 5 'A Chart of the Atlantic Ocean' from The West India Atlas by the late Thomas Jeffery. London, Sayer and Bennett, 1775. By courtesy of the Royal Geographical Society, London

Plate 6 The Illustrated London News *Coronation Special, 1902: map of the British Empire. Around the edge are the coats of arms of the various Dominions. By courtesy of the Mary Evans Picture Library*

Plate 7 'A network of dealing rooms that works for you round the clock'. By courtesy of Standard Chartered Bank/DMB & B Financial

Plate 8 Satellite image of the earth, centred on Africa. The picture is a composite created from thousands of separate images recorded by the Tiros-N series of meteorological satellites of NOAA. Each Tiros image was selected to show best the characteristics of a particular region. The chosen images were compiled into a vast database using a graphics supercomputer which then generated this composite. The picture is one of the results of the GeoSphere Project, created by Tom Van Sant in Santa Monica, California. By courtesy of Tom Van Sant/The GeoSphere Project, Santa Monica/Science Photo Library

Summary of section 2.1

o   To understand places and their local worlds it is necessary to
     imagine them in the web of connections that link them with other
     parts of the globe. 'Local worlds' cannot be understood outside
     their wider global connections.

o   Places are expressions of relations that are both social and spatial.
     A key to understanding places is to see them as being formed out
     of particular sets of social relations that interlock and interact at
     particular locations.

o   The social relations that constitute places are not all confined to
     them but are constructed and operate beyond them, connecting
     places and the people living in them to each other.

o   People construct and represent places and identify with them.
     Construction, representation and identification with place changes
     over time and may be contested.

2.2   Connecting 'local worlds'

2.2.1   'Triangular trade' connections: the black diaspora

The earliest connection between Liverpool and other local worlds shown in
Figure 2.1 is that made up by the so called 'Africa trade' or 'triangular trade'
of the seventeenth, eighteenth and early nineteenth centuries – the trade in
enslaved Africans that created the momentous black diaspora of world
history. The original biblical meaning of *diaspora* was the dispersal of Jewish   diaspora
peoples and the term has since been extended to signify the scattering of any
people from their 'original homelands' (however difficult it may be to
identify historically these origins). The enforced dispersal of enslaved
Africans has a history going back to the fifteenth century when European
traders brought a small number of enslaved Africans back to Europe. The
trade was gradually extended, initially by Spanish and Portuguese traders, to
islands in the Atlantic, the Caribbean and to South America. British, Dutch
and French traders soon joined, expanding the trade to the Caribbean and
to North America. The scattering of African people formed an integral part
of the global economic and political expansion of European states which was
revealed in the emergence of an interconnected, colonially-based global
economy. Potts (1990) refers to this colonial economy, and the black
diaspora on which it depended, as the first clear phase in the development
of a world market for labour power. Slaves were a key commodity in the
emerging global economy.

The geography of the triangular trade is shown in Figure 2.2 (see page 59).
The first leg of the journey involved ships sailing to Africa from Europe with
cargoes of manufactured goods – cloth (with cotton eventually replacing
wool), weapons, shoes, malt, spirits and brandy, pots and pans – which were
traded for slaves with dealers on arrival in Africa. The going rate for an
enslaved African male in 1801 is itemized, with an accountant's chilling eye
for detail, in Box 2.1.

Box 2.1 The price of a slave

'Paid for a Negro man at Bonny, in 1801:
One piece of Chintz, eighteen yards long.
One piece of Baft, eighteen yards long.
One piece of Chelloe, eighteen yards long.
One piece of Bandanoe, seven handkerchiefs.
One piece of Niccanee, fourteen yards long.
One piece of Photae, fourteen yards long
Three pieces of Romalls, forty-five handkerchiefs.
One large Brass Pan, two muskets.
Twenty-five kegs of powder, one hundred flints.
Two bags of shots, twenty knives.
Four iron pots, four hats, four caps.
Four cutlasses, six bunches of beads, fourteen gallons of brandy.
These articles cost about £25.'

Source: Williams, 1897, p. 680

The bartered slaves were then transported in conditions of unimaginable hardship (the infamous 'Middle Passage') to the Americas where they were sold to plantation owners. Receipts from these sales were then used to buy sugar, indigo and rum from the West Indies, or tobacco and, later, cotton from Virginia. These goods (or, in their stead, bills of exchange) were then transported back to Europe. Each leg of the voyage thus produced a trading profit. Accurate figures on the scale of the slave trade are difficult to come by but, between the middle of the fifteenth century and when the slave trade finally ended some four hundred years later, over ten million Africans were transported to the Americas. In addition, an estimated two million Africans never reached any of these destinations, having died from disease, suicide, murder or drowning following shipwreck during the 'Middle Passage'. As the trade developed, and as Britain extended its global power, Asia was added to this global network, with Indian manufacturing goods being gradually incorporated into the first leg of the journey (Cameron and Crooke, 1992). The Atlantic economy thus came to link together four continents in this particular phase of globalization – a massive global reach when one considers that the main form of transport and communication was by sail and sea.

Indeed, some historians have argued that for just over three centuries, starting with Christopher Columbus's first crossing of the Atlantic Ocean in 1492, a single 'Atlantic world' came into being. In this world the histories of Europe, America and Africa and the 'cultural hearths' of Europeans, Amerindians and Africans became inextricably linked (Karras and McNeill, 1992) (see Plate 5). And the central role of the black diaspora in this economic, political and cultural intermixing has been recognized by sociologists like Paul Gilroy who attempt to trace contemporary cultural developments to the period of the 'black Atlantic' (Gilroy, 1993; 1994).

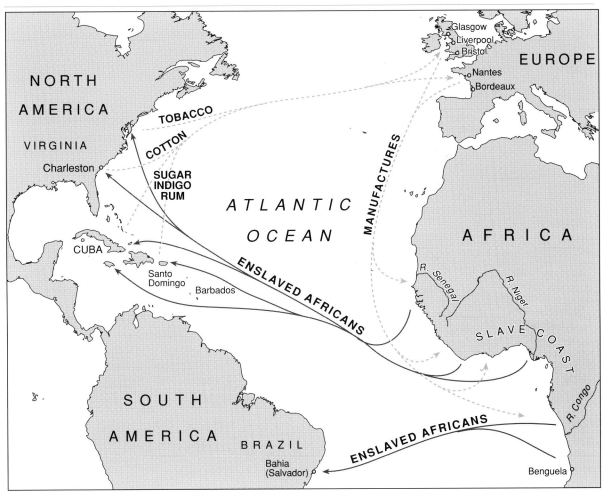

Figure 2.2 The triangular trade (seventeenth to nineteenth centuries) (Source: based on Knox and Agnew, 1994, Figure 9.3, p. 276)

For Africa, the economic, social, political and cultural legacies of the slave trade were momentous, leaving, in Patrick Manning's words, ' … Africans depleted in population, divided irremediably amongst themselves, retarded economically, and despised as an inferior race in a world which had built a vision of racial hierarchy based on the inspiration of their enslavement' (1992, p. 42). The history of North America has also been fundamentally shaped by the black diaspora – being scarred by civil war and struggles over black emancipation and assimilation, but also enriched by the cultural, social, economic and political contributions of slaves and their descendants.

The impact on Europe has been similarly momentous. Eric Williams (1944), for example, is convinced that the slave trade provided the capital on which European industrialization in general and that of Britain in particular were founded. Others, however, remain less sure, arguing that the profits from the trade could only have provided a relatively insignificant share of the total investment involved (Doyle, 1992), or that the role of the European domestic market was more important (Eltis, 1987). Eric Wolf is probably nearest to the mark when he argues that, while English industrial · development was not predicated mainly on the Atlantic trade, that trade did furnish English industrial development with a 'principal dynamic element' (1982, p. 200).

The impact of the slave trade on the 'local worlds' directly involved was certainly far-reaching. According to Eric Williams (1970), the experience of the West Indies as the 'cockpit of Europe' helped to create the islands as 'one world' – a fragmented, underdeveloped and unstable one. And Liverpool's early growth is inextricably bound up with the history of the West Indies and the American colonies. In the sixteenth century, the port's main trading links were with Ireland (a link we shall return to below) but, as Britain's colonies were developed in the late seventeenth and early eighteenth centuries, these links were extended across the Atlantic. The port's main cargoes in the mid-eighteenth to the early nineteenth centuries were salt (from Cheshire) and coal (from south-west Lancashire), and trade in these helped both to develop Liverpool's hinterland and to foster export markets in Europe, the Americas and the West Indies. At the same time, pressure for import trade developed markets in West Africa and the West Indies (with the latter being especially important for sugar). At the end of the eighteenth century, nearly four-fifths of Great Britain's overseas income came from the West Indies. Much of this will have come via Liverpool, and, of course, the euphemistically-titled 'Atlantic trade' was a key element in the increasing global reach of the port's merchant activities.

Liverpool was at the centre of Britain's colonial economy. This centrality – in relation specifically to the slave trade – is nicely, if bluntly, captured in the extract in Box 2.2 from *Sacred Hunger*, Barry Unsworth's Booker Prize-winning novel based on the slave trade. The speaker is a Liverpool merchant and shipowner (the fictional name of which, incidentally, is that of the first recorded slave ship to sail from Liverpool – the *Liverpool Merchant*).

Box 2.2 The geography of the slave trade and Liverpool's place in it

'The trade is wide open, I tell you, gentlemen. The colonies grow more populous by the year, by the month. The more land that is planted, the more they will want negroes. It is a case of first come, first served. And who is best placed to take it on? London is away there on the wrong side, with the Thames up her arse. Bristol's costs are twice ours here. I tell you, if God picked this town up in the palm of his hand and studied where best in England to set her down for the Africa trade, he would put her exactly back where she is, exactly where she stands at present.

He thumped his fist on the table so that the glasses rattled and sat looking round at the faces, challenging contradiction.'

Source: Unsworth, 1992, p. 15

In 1884, an account of Liverpool's participation in the 'Africa trade' was published in Liverpool with the front page shown in Figure 2.3. Revealingly, its author still felt it was necessary, 77 years after the abolition of the slave trade in Britain and 51 years after its abolition in the British Empire, to use the pseudonym 'Dicky Sam' (the Liverpudlian equivalent of a Cockney Londoner). The subject matter of the account was still clearly controversial and, as we shall see in section 2.3.1, has remained so to this day.

Consider the sentiments revealed in the 'old saying' quoted by Dicky Sam on that front page. It rather nicely, if crudely, captures just how important the Atlantic trade was to the traders and the town, and this importance was certainly corroborated by the figures exhaustively compiled by the 'eye-witness' that Dicky Sam cites in his account:

The following conclusions on the present state of the trade of Liverpool may be justly allowed by every impartial reader. First. That one-fourth of the ships belonging to the port of Liverpool are employed in the African trade. Second. That it has five-eighths of the African trade of Great Britain. Third. That it has three-sevenths of the African trade of all Europe.

Such is nearly the state of the general commerce of Liverpool, 1795.

(Dicky Sam, 1884, pp. 116–17)

It was those sentiments and those figures that helped to explain why local merchants, manufacturers and others with vested interests in the slave trade dedicated so much energy to fighting its proposed abolition. For them, there was no question but that abolition would mean ruin for the town.

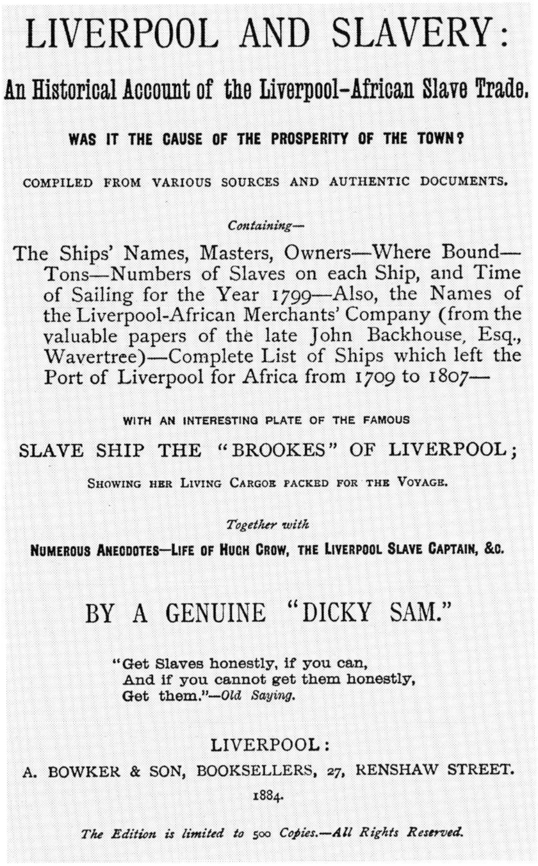

LIVERPOOL AND SLAVERY:

An Historical Account of the Liverpool-African Slave Trade.

WAS IT THE CAUSE OF THE PROSPERITY OF THE TOWN?

COMPILED FROM VARIOUS SOURCES AND AUTHENTIC DOCUMENTS.

Containing—

The Ships' Names, Masters, Owners—Where Bound—Tons—Numbers of Slaves on each Ship, and Time of Sailing for the Year 1799—Also, the Names of the Liverpool-African Merchants' Company (from the valuable papers of the late John Backhouse, Esq., Wavertree)—Complete List of Ships which left the Port of Liverpool for Africa from 1709 to 1807—

WITH AN INTERESTING PLATE OF THE FAMOUS

SLAVE SHIP THE "BROOKES" OF LIVERPOOL;

SHOWING HER LIVING CARGOE PACKED FOR THE VOYAGE.

Together with

NUMEROUS ANECDOTES—LIFE OF HUGH CROW, THE LIVERPOOL SLAVE CAPTAIN, &c.

BY A GENUINE "DICKY SAM."

"Get Slaves honestly, if you can,
And if you cannot get them honestly,
Get them."—*Old Saying.*

LIVERPOOL:

A. BOWKER & SON, BOOKSELLERS, 27, RENSHAW STREET.
1884.

The Edition is limited to 500 Copies.—All Rights Reserved.

Figure 2.3 The front page of Liverpool and Slavery, 1884

2.2.2 Connections of migration: the Irish diaspora

If the town's history is inextricably tied up with the 'black diaspora' of the slave trade, so too is it linked with another transatlantic diaspora – that of the Irish migration which stretched from the early seventeenth century to the establishment of the Irish Free State in 1922, and involved the movement of some seven million people from Ireland to North America (Miller, 1985). This migration peaked in the 1840s as economic and political factors encouraging migration were dramatically reinforced by the potato famine which literally starved people out of the country. Nearly one million of those seven million migrants travelled to the United States in the 1840s, 45 per cent of all the immigrants of that decade (National Geographic Society, 1988).

As already noted, Liverpool had longstanding links with Ireland and as the town grew it became a focus for Irish migrants, although the influx of Irish migrants did not really begin until the end of the eighteenth century (Parkinson, 1952). In 1800 there were five thousand Irish-born residents of the town and the next ten years saw this figure more than double to eleven thousand (Waller, 1981). Until then, the port had mainly been the final destination for the migrants or a gateway for onward migration to the industrializing North of England. Soon, however, these migrants became involved in another global flow with Liverpool at its centre. The cargo was again people, only this time the shackles were the psychological ones of economic and political exile. Moreover, the cargo physically moved through the town itself, unlike in the triangular trade, the geography of which meant that relatively few slaves actually reached Liverpool.

In the early 1820s, most Irish migrants to Canada and the United States sailed from Irish ports (especially Belfast, Dublin and Londonderry) but, as sailing links between Ireland and Britain and between the latter and the Americas developed and passage costs fell, Liverpool took over as a key port of departure. As early as 1826, one-third of Irish arrivals in New York had arrived via Liverpool (Miller, 1985). And Liverpool retained this leading role until direct steamship links between Ireland and the United States and Canada were established in the 1860s.

For a period of nearly four decades, then, Liverpool played a central role in the Irish diaspora, with a period in the 1840s of particularly intense activity marked by the onset in 1845 of the potato blight that turned into famine. The first three months of 1846 saw 90,000 Irish migrants arrive in the town while the second half of 1847 and the first half of 1848 saw another 300,000 flood in, an exodus which ' ... led to such turbulence that 20,000 townsmen had to be sworn in as special constables, and 2,000 regular troops camped at Everton' (Muir, 1907, p. 305). Neal (1988) estimates that something like 130,000 of the 1847 arrivals emigrated to the United States. Some will have moved on to other parts of Northern England while some will have stayed to add to the growing Irish-born population of the town which rose to nearly 84,000 in 1851. These figures meant, as Lawton and Pooley (1992) show, that in comparison with other British towns Liverpool housed, in absolute numbers, the second largest (behind London with nearly 109,000 Irish-born residents) and, in proportionate terms, the largest Irish community (at over 22 per cent of the total population).

THE EMBARKATION, WATERLOO DOCKS LIVERPOOL

'The Embarkation: Waterloo Docks, Liverpool': The 1850 date of this sketch of migrants embarking on their voyage from Liverpool to the 'New World' makes it extremely likely that most, in not all, of them were Irish

2.2.3 Indirect connections

The remaining link identified on Figure 2.1 is that between Liverpool and Rotterdam, a link of indirect connection. This is not to say that there have not been direct trading links of the kinds already discussed, but such direct links between the two ports have never been very important. Nor have the ports been in direct competition until relatively recently.

Rotterdam was settled much earlier than Liverpool, having reached Liverpool's population figure of the beginning of the eighteenth century two centuries earlier. In 1700 its population of 48,000 was six times that of Liverpool but, lacking the industrializing hinterland of Liverpool, its population quickly slipped behind as the industrialization of northern Europe and England in particular proceeded apace. By 1800 Rotterdam's population was under three-quarters that of Liverpool and by 1850 less than a third (de Vries, 1984). This reversal in importance of the two ports mirrors the similar national reversals in the relative power of England (Great Britain after the Acts of Union) and the Dutch republic. From being the greatest commercial and naval power in Europe in the middle of the seventeenth century, the Dutch republic had been overtaken in both areas by Great Britain in the first quarter of the eighteenth century (Doyle, 1992). Britain's lead in industrialization and its rapidly growing Empire reinforced this position. Britain became the 'workshop of the world' and leading imperial power in the nineteenth century, and it was Liverpool which served this workshop and acted as 'gateway' to this Empire – a global role and significance which overshadowed Rotterdam and other ports on the European continent.

An early indication of the relative status of the two ports is indicated by their differing participation in the 'Atlantic trade'. Apart from brief periods in the seventeenth century, the Dutch never played a major role in it, perhaps accounting overall for around 5 per cent of the total number of slaves involved. And if there was a Dutch equivalent of Liverpool it was not Rotterdam but the island of Walcheren in the province of Zeeland. Rotterdam, which was involved in the slave trade through the Maze Chamber of the Dutch West Indies Company, was ranked third in importance in slave trading after Zeeland and Amsterdam (Postma, 1990).

The late nineteenth century, however, saw the first signs of change. The provision of a new short waterway to the sea in 1872 facilitated the growth of Rotterdam which, by the end of the century, had reinforced its position as second city of the Netherlands. But it was not until after the Second World War that Rotterdam really began to grow in relative importance. Large amounts of state money were invested in developing the port's facilities (Pollock, 1981), and these investments in changing port technology and in road, rail and inland waterway links with a developing continental hinterland have seen Rotterdam become a leading European and world port (Hayuth and Hilling, 1992). And while Rotterdam has risen in the league of seaports, Liverpool has slid down it – as a result of Britain's relative decline as a trading nation, the deindustrialization of the port's hinterland and its westward-facing orientation in relation to Britain's trading and geopolitical shift eastwards to Europe. Figure 2.4 shows the location of the two seaport cities in the 'New Europe'. Rotterdam is located in the 'backbone' of growth (often referred to as the 'blue banana' because of its shape and colouring on the map on which it first appeared – another example of the 'power of maps'!), while Liverpool is marooned on the 'margins'.

Rotterdam's key role in the emerging 'Single European Market' is revealed particularly clearly in the emerging geography of seaborne container cargoes. Given the increasing size of container ships, to minimize costs shipowners have cut back on the number of ports that these massive ships call in to. A small number of 'direct call' ports serve 'feeder ports' (Hayuth and Hilling, 1992). Direct call ports include Bremerhaven in Germany, Le Havre in France, Antwerp in Belgium, Felixstowe in the UK – and, in the Netherlands, Rotterdam. As the world's largest deep-sea port, Rotterdam is attempting to become the leading European port by, for example, developing large distribution centres ('Distriparks') providing warehousing and storage, processing facilities and transport links that it hopes will make it the new 'gateway to Europe' (Hayuth and Hilling, 1992, p. 53). The contrast with Liverpool could not be much clearer: a former 'gateway to Empire' now competing with the potential 'gateway to Europe'.

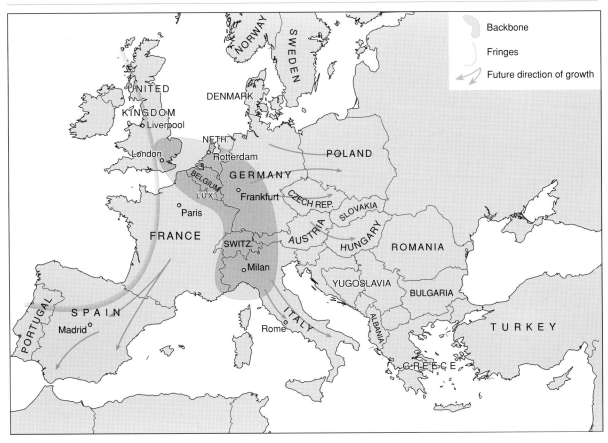

Figure 2.4 The New Europe

Summary of section 2.2

The main aim of section 2.2 was to show that to understand 'local worlds' it is necessary to explore the historical evolution and nature of their interconnections with other places. To illustrate this, three examples of Liverpool's global connections were described:

o   its involvement in the black diaspora through its key role in the Atlantic slave trade;

o   its involvement in the Irish diaspora, serving as both a final destination and stopping-off point for Irish migration;

o   its historical relationship with another important northern European port, Rotterdam.

In section 2.3, I want to take the account a step further by focusing more closely on Liverpool, and, taking in turn each of these historical connections, attempt to suggest ways in which the town's connections with other 'local worlds' have helped not only to shape its economic, social, cultural and political life but also to influence the way in which it has been represented by both 'insiders' and 'outsiders'.

2.3   Local worlds: constitution and reconstitution

2.3.1   The 'triangular trade' and Liverpool

The 'triangular trade' undeniably played a crucial role in Liverpool's development. In the first place, the trade gave an important kickstart to the growth of the town's global oceanic trading activities. Secondly, it served to establish trading patterns and connections which foreshadowed subsequent ones that were to prove crucial once the slave trade was abolished. Thirdly, the trade contributed to the development of local activities supplying the slave ships and processing some of the commodities brought back on the third leg of the journey. Fourthly, it established global connections which encouraged the voluntary flow of migrants who were to reshape the town's social structure and geography. Finally, it was an important influence on the way in which the town was represented in its formative years – a representation which has cast shadows that remain controversial to this day.

Dicky Sam quoted figures showing that, in just eleven years at the height of a trade in which Liverpool was involved for just over a century, an annual net profit of approximately £214,678 was recouped by Liverpool slave traders and associated investors. When the first recorded slave ship, the *Liverpool Merchant*, set out on its journey in 1700 the port had about 70 ships. Half a century later this number had more than tripled (to 220), and nearly a quarter (53) had left the port to engage in the 'Africa trade'. The number of ships registered in the port continued to increase as the century closed, while the proportion of ships engaged in the 'Africa trade' declined. In 1801, six years before abolition, 122 ships cleared for the 'Africa trade', just 15 per cent of the total of 821 ships clearing the port. But if anything revealed the importance of the trade to the port it was the strength of the lobby that was mobilized to oppose abolition. As Cameron and Crooke point out:

Whilst towns and counties throughout the country flooded Parliament with petitions calling for the abolition of the trade, Liverpool dispatched a total of 64 petitions defending the trade in the years 1788–1807. (In the same period London sent 14 petitions in defence of the trade, and Bristol 12.) Not a single petition in opposition to the trade emanated from Liverpool. Whilst over 20,000 of Manchester's population of 75,000 signed a mass petition against the slave trade, Liverpool's leading citizens drank toasts on the king's birthday to 'Prosperity to the African trade, and may it always be conducted with humanity'.

(Cameron and Crooke, 1992, p. 44)

Note the tension that this quotation reveals between Liverpool and the town with which it had an almost umbilical – if unwelcome and uncomfortable – connection: Manchester. We shall return to this tension below.

We have already seen how Dicky Sam was very keen to preserve his (or her?) anonymity. Memories of the rough treatment that Clarkson, the great anti-slavery campaigner, had received on his visit to Liverpool and the physical assault on William Roscoe, the town's short-lived MP who had the temerity to vote in Parliament in favour of abolition, clearly lingered long. The role of the city in the slave trade was a subject that was best left alone.

In fact, however, the eventual abolition of the slave trade did little to curtail the growth of trade and the town. New commodities more than made up for its loss. Trade in one of the key commodities, cotton, had been promoted by the Atlantic trade, alongside sugar and rum. And this commodity – still produced by the slaves of the black diaspora and their descendants – soon dominated the town's trade, only this time it actually passed through it. As Frank Musgrove stresses in his history of the North of England, it was an *international* trade with profound implications for the *local* worlds involved:

The international connections of cotton were important not simply for the economy of England and Lancashire. They shaped an outlook and fashioned a new, forward-looking northern society. Cotton revivified the civilization of the North in a way comparable to the international connections of monasticism in the age of Bede. It was more potent even than wool exports in the thirteenth century, which secured prosperity for eastern Yorkshire and an active place in a vigorous North Sea civilization. Lancashire was now an Atlantic state.

(Musgrove, 1990, p. 261)

And Liverpool was once again a key location in this global network of trade and production linking the Southern States of the US with India and Egypt and, for a short period, Brazil and, later, Uganda (see Figure 2.5). In the nineteenth century, 'King Cotton' dominated the town's trade and bolstered its importance in the national economy. During this period the port was responsible for between 80 and 90 per cent of the country's imports of this world-changing commodity (Hyde, 1971). Africa was also the source of new products – most notably in the case of Liverpool, palm oil which was used in the manufacture of soap, lubricants and candles (Hopkins, 1973). Liverpool merchants came to dominate the delta of the River Niger and yet another link, this time in so-called 'legitimate trades', was made with Africa – a link

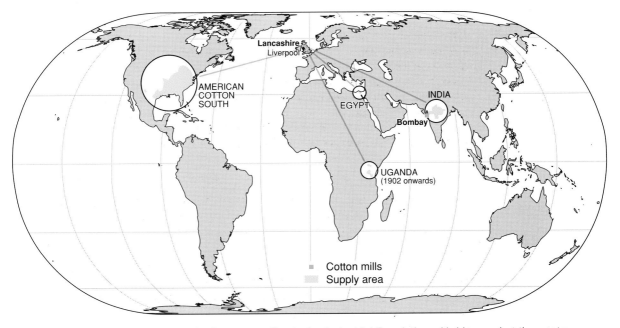

Figure 2.5 Manufacture and supply of cotton textiles in the Industrial Revolution with Liverpool at the centre (Source: based on Wolf, 1982, p. 279)

to which the growth on Merseyside, for example, of Lever Brothers' giant soap and margarine business and the Elder Dempster shipping company can be directly traced (Davies, 1973).

The dock system expanded in line with the expansion of trade throughout the nineteenth and early twentieth centuries, and a whole range of processing and port-related industries was established. In the period between the two World Wars, when the city was probably at the peak of its global economic importance, there were 90 docks, with warehouse accommodation for 500,000 tons of cargo, handling 15 million tons of traffic a year. In the same period, industries in the town and its immediate outskirts included flour milling (the second largest milling centre in the world), shipbuilding and ship repairing, tobacco (the largest tobacco warehouse in the world) and sugar processing (both of the latter still surviving from the old triangular trade links with the Americas). Nearby was the largest soap works in the country sustained by its links with West Africa (Liverpool City Council, 1930).

Banking in the town can also trace its roots back to the triangular trade and the bills of exchange that were brought back from America:

The developments in banking were more significant. The earliest Liverpool bankers were merchants who grafted banking onto their other commercial activities. More and more slave-trading merchants in particular were drawn into banking, as the number of slaves paid for by bills of exchange drawn on English merchants increased in the latter half of the eighteenth century.

Arthur Heywood and Charles Caldwell were the first slave traders to move into banking in the 1770s, quickly followed by William Gregson, Thomas Staniforth and Joseph Daltera. In 1802 Leyland became a partner in Liverpool's oldest bank, first established by William Clarke in 1774. In later years Gregson's bank was to be absorbed by the Bank of Liverpool, in turn

City of Empire: Liverpool's famous waterfront buildings (from left to right) – Liver Building, Cunard Building and former headquarters of the Mersey Docks and Harbour Board. Built between 1907 and 1917, they symbolize the city's historic importance globally and testify to the city's own recognition of that importance

absorbed by Barclay's, whilst Leyland's bank was to be absorbed by the North and South Wales Bank, in turn absorbed by the Midland. By the turn of the century ten of the fourteen most prominent bankers in Liverpool had progressed into banking from the slave trade: the Heywood brothers, the Staniforth brothers, Gregson, Leyland, Daltera, Ingram, Bold and Harly.

(Cameron and Crooke, 1992, p. 30)

The town's connections with other places across the globe could thus clearly be seen in its very built environment – its docks, its warehouses, its factories, its banks and office buildings. The links between this built environment and the slave trade in particular were perhaps most famously – and, in the circumstances, bravely – expressed by an actor whom Dicky Sam could not resist quoting:

Memorable are the cutting words of George Frederick Cooke, tragedian, born seventeenth April, 1756, died 26th September, 1812. At the Liverpool Theatre one night, as was usual on many occasions with him, he staggered on the stage drunk; when the audience perceived this, they loudly hissed and hooted at him. Cooke steadying himself, shouted most vociferously, I have not come here to be insulted by a set of wretches, of which every brick in your infernal town is cemented with an African's blood.

(Dicky Sam, 1884, pp. 15–16)

The town's global connections – those particular social relationships stretched across the globe – helped to make it unique, and this uniqueness found powerful expression in its built environment.

What also stands out in the development of the town's uniqueness is the way in which the economic and political lives of the town were fused together:

37 of the 41 members of Liverpool Council in 1787 were involved in the slave trade in one way or another, as too were all 20 mayors who held office between 1787 and 1807. With the brief exception of Roscoe in the period 1806–07, all Liverpool MPs of the eighteenth and early nineteenth centuries were either slave traders in their own right or defenders of the trade in Parliament. Liverpool was not just the economic capital of the slave trade. It was also its political capital.

(Cameron and Crooke, 1992, p. 24)

The single-minded defence of its interests in the slave trade (which went so far as rewarding a Jesuit priest for producing a pamphlet arguing that slavery did not go against the teachings of the Bible) set the town apart. Abolitionists were in a very visible, and threatened, minority. This had important implications for the representation of the town to both insiders and outsiders. It marked the beginning of a long history of the townspeople defining themselves in opposition to others – by what they were not, as well as by what they were, and in relation to other local worlds to which they were opposed.

This self-definition in opposition to others can perhaps be most clearly seen in Liverpool's attitudes towards, and rivalry with, the town with which it has had almost a symbiotic relationship since England's colonial expansion and industrialization – Manchester.

The relationship between the two places – one a commercial centre of a manufacturing region requiring access to the world for the raw materials and manufactured produce that it handled, the other a port needing commodities to trade – was always going to be strained. The tensions between mercantilist and manufacturing interest and the associated social distinctions are famously captured in the nineteenth-century comparison between 'Liverpool Gentlemen and Manchester Men' (I shall return to the gendering of this comparison below). And these tensions certainly revealed themselves in the differing stances taken by the two towns towards slavery: the port clinging to the trade, the manufacturing town opposing it not simply on humanitarian grounds but also because it represented what it saw as a mercantile anachronism and an obstacle to the development of the *laissez-faire* capitalism which would assure its future. The characterization of the pro- and anti-slavery debates in Parliament between 'Liverpool Men' and 'Humanity Men' (there were, of course no women in Parliament at this time) does tend to gloss over the economic interests underpinning them.

The tension between the towns has persisted to this day and, as we shall see in section 2.4, is particularly visible at the time of writing in relation to the development of the two towns' airports. Historically, the tension was to do with the seaport. From the port's earliest days the question of the non-payment of dock dues by Liverpool freemen (freewomen were not allowed) had rankled with other users of the port, especially when the dues did not always appear to be going back into the improvement of the port's facilities. The appointment of a small number of dock ratepayers to the Trustees of Liverpool Docks in 1825 did not assuage these fears and opposition to the privileges of Liverpool freemen continued to grow. The most powerful opposition came from Manchester, whose Chamber of Commerce and Commercial Association allied with the Great Western Railway to demand the creation of a body controlled by dock users, with the right to collect dues and manage the docks (Marriner, 1982; Mountfield, 1965). Box 2.3 gives a flavour of the feelings in Liverpool about this intervention, as revealed in the debates over the Parliamentary Bill that finally established the Mersey Docks and Harbour Board in 1857. Note, in particular, the statement linking the prosperity of both Liverpool and Manchester to their global connections.

Box 2.3 A Liverpool view of Manchester (1857)

'Its (Manchester's) Municipal body finds that it cannot vie with that at Liverpool and it seems determined, therefore, to spare no efforts to bring down the Corporation of Liverpool to its own level. For several years past no opportunity has been lost of discussing the question of the Liverpool Town Dues in the Town Council of Manchester ... and an agitation has been got up throughout the manufacturing districts of Lancashire and Yorkshire to deprive the Corporation of Liverpool of those dues. Public meetings have been held and speeches delivered displaying a great amount of ignorance on the subject and a bitter feeling of hostility to Liverpool and her dues ...

Sir, Manchester says it has made Liverpool. Sir, the East and West Indies, America and Africa and Australia have made Liverpool, just as they have made Manchester.

What is the next thing? It is to pull down Liverpool, to make Liverpool forsooth the Piraeus of such an Athens as Manchester.'

Source: quoted in Mountfield, 1965, pp. 9 and 12

While the creation of the Mersey Docks and Harbour Board, against Liverpool's strenuous opposition, did go some way towards meeting the objections of Manchester, concern about the charges for use of the dock, congestion and the railway companies' monopoly of land carriage of cargoes persisted (Marriner, 1982). Box 2.4 contains an extract from an article in the *Manchester Evening News* in 1883 which gave vent to these views, complaining bitterly about the 'Toll Bar' that Liverpool had allegedly erected to Manchester enterprise. Note again, the importance of place representation in the argument – Slocum Pogis and all that it represents may be bad but Liverpool is far worse.

Lateral thinking in the end provided the answer: Manchester needed its own port. And, once again in the face of vehement opposition from Liverpool, Manchester lobbied for, and finally gained, Parliamentary approval in 1887 for the construction of the Manchester Ship Canal which linked the town directly to the River Mersey and the Irish Sea.

Box 2.4 A Manchester view of Liverpool (1883)

'The gentlemen who compose the Mersey Docks and Harbour Board, and who graciously allow us to make use of a river which nature especially provided for them and the dwellers thereon as an inheritance for ever, are all gentlemen of the highest respectability, who perform a great public duty for nothing … (Ahem!) … The fact that they and their predecessors have during the last fifty years taxed our trade to the amount of £9,000,000 in town dues alone, gives us no say in the matter at all. Who are the men who invented the mule and the loom, the steam engine and a few little oddments of that sort, that have revolutionized the world? Pygmies, Sir, pygmies as compared with our friends of the Docks Board.

"One dog, one bone" has been Liverpool's motto and no little pettifogging tradesman in Slocum Pogis was ever so jealous of his neighbour as Liverpool has been.'

Source: quoted in Mountfield, 1965, pp. 12 and 56

I would argue that these early battles with Manchester – and all the economic, political, social and cultural relationships that were bound up in them – helped to 'make' Liverpool by reinforcing its apartness, its difference, its uniqueness. It is worth recalling here just how out of step the town was in its pro-slavery stance. As Linda Colley points out in her (1992) book on the 'invention' of Britain and the formation of British national identity, *Britons: Forging the Nation 1707–1837*, the mass-petitioning against the slave trade initiated by Manchester in 1788 was soon followed by another hundred towns, which made the public petitioning campaign the largest organized in Britain to that date. The Liverpool supporters of the slave trade at that time were very visibly running against the grain of what was becoming national public opinion. Liverpool was defining itself, and representing itself, in relation to this opposition. It was only when the predicted dire consequences of the loss of the slave trade failed to materialize after abolition that the town fell into line with public opinion on one of the three key issues that Colley argues were vital in the creation of British identity after 1815 (the other two issues being Catholic emancipation and the extension of the franchise).

If early representations of the town were about establishing difference and uniqueness, they also shared another common feature – one often reinforced by the representations of historians – they were predominantly masculine. The town's affairs were run by 'Liverpool Gentlemen' and 'Merchant Princes' who gave the town its pretensions to culture while the comings and goings of male seafarers and their behaviour in port gave the town a widely recognized image of vitality and toughness. In his rather feeble attempts to deal with the slave trade in his history of the port, Parkinson (1952) talks about the 'special toughness in the Liverpool fibre' and how: 'We need not be unduly ashamed of our ancestors who sailed in the Guineamen (slave ships). They were no worse than their neighbours and in one respect they were better; for we know at least that they were *men*' (quoted in Cameron and Crooke, 1992, p.69). Joseph Conrad, remembering a particular Liverpool ship, evoked this image of toughness far more eloquently: 'That crew of Liverpool hard cases had in them the right stuff. It's my experience they always have' (quoted in Lane, 1987).

The representation of the 'local world' thus had a masculine edge to it which in many respects has persisted to this day, with dockers and car workers and more recently militant male local government workers taking the place of seafarers in press and broadcast media images of the town's 'maleness'. Reading A, an extract from the conclusions of Linda Grant's writing on *Women Workers and the Sexual Division of Labour: Liverpool 1890–1939*, gives a rather different historical picture.

Activity 2 Now read Reading A by Linda Grant, entitled 'Women workers and the sexual division of labour: Liverpool 1890–1939', which you will find at the end of this chapter. As you read, reflect on some of the main points she is attempting to make:

o The role of local economic conditions and traditions in creating a sexual division of labour: the way in which the 'casualism' of a segment of the local labour market deemed to be 'male' helped to structure another segment deemed 'female'.

o The notion of women's work being 'hidden work': given the fact that personal services were of nearly equal numerical importance in terms of job numbers as dock work, why has the sector never been recognized historically as being of equal importance in 'defining/representing' the town?

o The ways in which cultural attitudes and consciousness in relation to notions of masculinity and femininity are translated into employment structures which, in turn, feed back into that consciousness.

o The relationship between local and wider factors in shaping the local gender division of labour.

Liverpool's global trading connections also had important implications for the town in the way in which they encouraged the flow of people and migrants. Only a small number of Africans were brought to the city for sale. The economics of the triangular trade clearly discouraged such a pattern. The domestic market for slaves was relatively limited and the arrival of slaves in Liverpool in any great number would have meant that a significant tier of the journey's profit cake had been forgone. Nevertheless, the African connections developed by the slave trade and the 'legitimate trade' that superseded it did lay the foundations, however fragile, for the gradual development in Liverpool of a black population that consisted of freed slaves (some of whom possibly fought on Britain's side in the American War of Independence), servants of plantation owners and merchants, the children of West African chiefs sent for education and, especially, West African seafarers who settled in the town. At first, most of the migrants clustered in the centre of the city close to the docks, but then they gradually moved a short distance outwards to an area that in the middle of the nineteenth century had been parkland inhabited by wealthy merchants, known then as Toxteth Park (van Helmond and Palmer, 1991).

Thus, one key element of the black diaspora's legacy for Liverpool was the creation of a 'local world' within a 'local world': an increasingly geographically and socially segregated black community. This *social and spatial segregation* was encouraged by racially-motivated rioting in 1919 and 1948, when black residents became the targets of mob violence. And, as the last Census of Population in 1991 showed, it has persisted, with just three of the city's thirty-three census wards containing over 40 per cent of its black population. The degree of social disadvantage experienced by the black population was also revealed in the Census figures, with black residents having an unemployment rate of 27 per cent compared with the white population's rate of 21 per cent. The difference was even higher for unemployment amongst black and white youth, with the rate for the former being 40 per cent and that for the latter 31 per cent (Liverpool City Council, 1993). These depressing figures, it should be remembered, were recorded some ten years after the explosion of anger and frustration amongst black and white youth that resulted in a summer of riots across Britain. And, as Peter Fryer points out: 'With remarkable historical symmetry, this burst of youthful rage began, and proved to be most powerful and sustained, in the very cities which had once been this country's chief slave ports: Bristol, London and Liverpool' (Fryer, 1984, p. 399).

social and spatial segregation

The riots in 'Liverpool 8' (or as it is still known outside the city and in the media, 'Toxteth') violently underscored the local geography of discrimination and disadvantage. Lord Scarman, appointed to inquire into the Brixton riots in London, travelled to Liverpool and found this geography – and the social, economic cultural and political forces helping to shape it – especially worrying: 'One finds in Toxteth, which is a tiny area, a black community largely confined to that tiny area … I won't use the word which obviously comes to one's lips, but that community has got to get into the rest of Liverpool and the rest of Liverpool has got to receive it' (quoted in the *Liverpool Echo*, 25 November, 1981). He clearly felt that a part of the 'local world' had become 'disconnected', both economically and socially.

A significant proportion of black people in Liverpool are concerned that there is still a long way to go before such a geographical and social reconciliation can be achieved, given what they see as the deeply entrenched and historically-rooted racism endemic in the city. This racism and its historical roots provided the theme of a BBC Radio 4 programme, 'Slave City First', broadcast on 29 April, 1993. A central criticism concerned the lack of any permanent exhibition in the city's award-winning Maritime Museum of the town's involvement in the slave trade and the black diaspora (whereas, for example, a major exhibition of the flow of migrants through the town was long established). The city, it was argued, was sanitizing its history.

Cameron and Crooke (1992) have argued that historians of the city – especially 'official historians' – have proved to be particularly adept at distancing it from its activities in the slave trade. There are a number of honourable exceptions to this rule (Muir, 1907 being a particularly notable one), but it is generally the case that historians when dealing with the issue have tended to emphasize the unfairness of the city being singled out for criticism when other towns were involved, and/or the relative insignificance of the trade in relation to the port's other trading activities.

To its credit, the Maritime Museum at the time of writing is in the process of establishing a permanent gallery on the slave trade, entitled 'Transatlantic slavery: against human dignity', sponsored by a grant from a local charitable foundation (the Peter Moores Foundation). The gallery's declared statement of intent is to '… increase public understanding of the experience of Black people in Britain and the modern world through an examination of the Atlantic slave trade and the African Diaspora' (National Museums and Galleries on Merseyside, *Progress Report and Background Information*, June 1994). As the declaration of intent indicates and briefing documents support, the emphasis of the gallery is on a national perspective. But if the gallery does its job correctly – and the signs so far are that it will do so very effectively – it will surely demonstrate the difficulties of separating the national from the local. The obvious point here, of course, is that, in the second half of the eighteenth century, Liverpool unquestionably dominated Britain's slave-trading activities. The local was very much the national. But the national was also the local when, as has been argued, the town was defining itself in opposition to national public opinion over proposed abolition of the trade. Its local stance was conditioned, in part, by national opinion. Moreover, Liverpool's abolitionists, albeit small in number, were acting on both a local and a national stage in their attempts to persuade both local people and national legislators of the merits of their case. Their efforts were *simultaneously* local and national.

2.3.2   The Irish diaspora and Liverpool

Like the black migrants to Liverpool, the Irish moved initially into areas close to the docks and, like the black migrants, created districts which fitted into an overall mosaic in which ethnic distinction was important: '… whole areas *belonged* to the Catholic Irish, the Protestant Irish and the Welsh' (Smith, 1986, p. 171). Another international triangular pattern of interconnection – the so-called 'industrial triangle of Belfast, Liverpool and Glasgow' – helped to shape this geography, with Irish and Scottish Protestants moving into the town and forming an Orange Order as early as 1819 (Davis, 1991). With the influx of rural, predominantly Roman Catholic Irish migrants with the 'famines' of the 1840s, the stage was clearly set for communal strife (Belchem, 1992).

The Scotland Road ('Scotty Road' in local parlance), running parallel with the river about a mile inland in the 'North End' of the city, provided both an important boundary (containing, on its river side, a predominantly Irish Roman Catholic community) and a stage on which religious and sectarian division was played out. Box 2.5 gives a flavour of just how tightly knit these local worlds within local worlds actually were. It is taken from Pat Ayers's history of one part of Liverpool's docklands that was known locally as 'Over the Bridge'.

Activity 3 Read Box 2.5 and note the tightly constrained social geographies of local communities like 'Over the Bridge', in which very clear distinctions between 'insiders' and 'outsiders' were drawn.

Drawing where possible on your own experiences, make up a checklist of the benefits and disbenefits of this form of *localism*.

localism

Box 2.5 'Over the Bridge'

'Athol Street is situated in the north end of Liverpool and runs down between Scotland Road and Great Howard Street. Although intersected by Vauxhall Road and the viaduct which carries the Liverpool to Southport railway line, it is the Leeds/Liverpool canal which provides the main divide and sets apart the area over the bridge from the top end – a division which endures both for those who still live there and in the memories of those who have left; if they said, "Where do you live?" you said, "Over the Bridge".

In many ways, of course, Over the Bridge is very like other dockland areas. People generally saw themselves as part of a particular locality, often identifying this around parish, school or industry. All the basic needs of family, work, education, shopping, leisure and health care, were provided in the immediate area so there was little need for people to travel outside the security of familiar neighbourhoods. On top of this there was an expectation that children born and reared Over the Bridge would stay there after they left school, went to work and married: "You stayed in your own community … It was a sacrilege to marry out of Over the Bridge." Local people still speak in awe of a couple who married before the War and moved away: "I never could understand it, why they did that. He'd been abroad and all that but they belonged down here. I mean they'd not, especially her, known different. I still think they took a chance." If people weren't expected to move away, neither were newcomers expected to move in. "Outsiders" remained outsiders in collective memories even twenty or thirty years after they had come to live in the area: "Over the Bridge my mother was never accepted … I remember just before we left in about 1965, she had a big row with … in the street and she said, 'Eh well, you were never welcome here anyway, you up-the-road tart.'" '

Source: Ayers, 1990, pp. 2–4

Distinctions were also drawn on religious grounds and, as Pat Ayers goes on to argue, religious difference in these communities became particularly important on days of celebration – for Protestants the twelfth of July, for Catholics St Patrick's Day – and were usually translated into violence (see Box 2.6).

Box 2.6 Which side are you on?

'Oh God, it was terrible, absolutely dreadful. We used to stand out by that railway bridge, in Athol Street and throw stones as they were going to Southport. You know, on the twelfth of July, they [the Orange Lodge] used to go to Southport, always and ever. They all had beautiful clothes on, for the times, like they do now. And as the trains would be going past, of course they knew it was a Catholic area, they'd throw all the lemonade bottles and everything out through the train windows. Needless to say, night-time, when they were coming back there'd be retaliations.'

'Retaliation' could take various forms:

'… But, don't forget, at the other end, Over the Bridge, they weren't without their little doings as well. They'd have King Billy on a big rope on the twelfth of July and string it across Athol Street. And as soon as the train'd get near, they'd set fire to it and then all the bottles would come out.'

Particularly defiant provocation was offered annually by a woman who lived in rooms over a chip shop in Athol Street:

'... her window overlooked the railway line. And every year without fail, every one of her windows went in. Because she was Irish, her name was Nan H. She looked out of her window and the railway tracks ran underneath. And she used to put the yellow, green and white flag out and of course, she paid the penalty every year. But she didn't care. She got every window put in.'

Source: Ayers, 1990, p. 58

There were particularly serious outbreaks of sectarian rioting in 1850 and 1909, which set Liverpool very markedly apart on mainland Britain (Bohstedt, 1992). A number of academics have explored the reasons why Liverpool was much more prone to religious rioting than other towns with large Irish communities, especially that other mainland point of the 'industrial triangle', Glasgow (see, for example, Gallagher, 1985; Smith, 1984 and 1986). The answer lies in the particular constitution of Liverpool's 'local world'. One important dimension of this was the residential segregation on ethnic lines already described. Box 2.7 gives a couple of views on how this segregation was both constituted by and helped to constitute politics in the city.

Box 2.7 Religious divisions

'Protestant politics in Liverpool were more volatile because religious affiliation was at the heart of political and social life to a greater degree than in Glasgow. Liverpool's residential segregation along religious lines was far more complete than Glasgow's, where no districts were exclusively populated by Catholic immigrants. In Liverpool in 1909, riots over religious processions led to hundreds of families fleeing the districts in which they were a religious minority. The chief instigator of this sectarian warfare was pastor George Wise ... During the early 1900s he exemplified *the importance of territoriality in the ordinary social relations of Liverpool,* by holding processions in an area where the Catholic bishop's residence, two convents and three churches were sited.'

Source: Gallagher, 1985, p. 114; my emphasis

'The sectarian rioting in 1909 dwarfed anything seen in the city in the nineteenth century. These eruptions also can be misleadingly titled. Some might argue, as others in the past did, that what was done in the name of religion was atrocious enough to be called pagan and to warrant more rather than less missionary work from the churches. The tensions in Liverpool society, which were manifested in its politics, stemmed not simply from genuine or bastard religiosity, but also from the tendencies towards heterogeneity in that society. National distinctiveness and separate cultural ties were not dissolved and effaced in a melting pot, but sustained by neighbourhood warmth and perpetuated by education over generations. Not that the country Irish or the country Welsh, to take the largest alien groups who settled in Liverpool, remained absolutely as before, impervious to their adopted city. *A reconstitution did occur, but this new growth was a hybrid, with singular and common traits, which left the Liverpool Irish and the Liverpool Welsh still shaped as identifiable groups.'*

Source: Waller, 1981, p. xvii; my emphasis

One factor which most clearly distinguishes Liverpool from other cities in the North of England was the relatively late development there of the Labour Party. While a number of Labour Party candidates were elected to Parliament in the 1920s, it was not until 1955 that the Labour Party managed to gain control of a city with an industrial structure and socio-economic composition which in other places had provided a fertile base for the development of the Labour Party vote. In Liverpool, the Tories took control of the council and retained control, apart from a very brief period (1892–5), for over a century. To understand why, it is necessary to understand how Liverpool's 'local world' was constituted over time and how this process of constitution was itself linked with processes and social relationships operating at a national level.

Let us take a look at some of the key ingredients in this mix. An essential one was the particular structure of the local labour market. It was dominated by two occupations, both heavily dependent on patronage and difficult to organize: casual work on the waterfront (largely classified as unskilled and paid accordingly), and clerical work. Both had hierarchies of status and it was the relatively low status, casual and low-paid jobs for which the Irish migrants were best able to compete (Gallagher, 1985; Smith 1984 and 1986). The casual work on the docks in particular, where men had to congregate daily at 'stands' to be picked for work, encouraged individualism and the various job specialisms in dock work (described by one observer at the end of the nineteenth century as a 'caste system quite as powerful as India's') that fragmented the workforce and inhibited the wider development of both trade unionism and the Labour Party vote. A further divisive factor was social-spatial segregation on religious grounds, with the north end of the dock system dominated by Catholic dockers and the south end by Protestants. While there were no serious instances of sectarian violence on the waterfront – these were concentrated on the boundaries of the districts where the two groups were housed, as described by Pat Ayers above – religious division still operated as a potentially divisive factor undermining attempts to build union and political representation (Taplin, 1986). Segregation in the housing market on religious grounds was thus mirrored by segregation in a major segment of the local labour market. The local world was itself fragmented into smaller local worlds within it.

Another important ingredient related to the structure of the local labour market was the lack of a strong cooperative movement or friendly societies that could provide the bases for an organized labour movement. The absence of a skilled working class to organize such societies, and the predominance of casual, irregular wages meant that, in Liverpool, much greater resort was made to 'money' and 'burial' clubs, moneylenders and pawnbrokers. Also important were the 'tontines' that required shorter-term payments and had earlier divisions of these payments than did the fellowship societies more usual among the working class at this time – arrangements which clearly more suited a casual workforce. But again what was also important about these tontines was the way in which they were attached to political organizations and churches, thus '... reinforcing and helping to recreate ethnic and religious differences' (Smith, 1986, p. 174).

Throw into this mixture, then, political parties organized around militant Protestantism, on the one hand, and Home Rule for Ireland, on the other, and it is possible to understand why Liberalism withered on the local political vine and why the Independent Labour Party had difficulty in establishing itself.

As far as Protestant workers were concerned, the Liberals were tainted by their support of Home Rule for Ireland. The 'Tory Democracy' on offer was infinitely more attractive, with its stance against Catholicism and Home Rule for Ireland and its militant support of the established churches and the Constitution. A distinctive strand of working-class Conservatism was thus created out of this mix of local and national factors – epitomized by the city's Working Men's (*sic*) Conservative Association which, with its mixing of political and leisure activities, became a formidable, and unique, political force in mobilizing the Protestant working-class vote. In contrast, why should Catholic workers bother with the Liberals (who tended to be non-conformist in religious outlook) or any nascent socialist party, even if both professed to support Home Rule for Ireland, when there was an established party organized around this very issue – the Irish National League (United Irish League after 1898) – which was the mirror image of the loyal Protestantism of the Working Men's Conservative Association and local Tory Party machine?

It was this divided local world which produced, on the one hand, a century of Tory control of the local council and, on the other, the only Irish Nationalist MP elected outside of Ireland (T.P. O'Connor). Joan Smith (1986) sums up Liverpool's local political world as a 'Conservative local state based on sectarianism' and one which contrasted markedly with the 'Liberal local state' that was constructed at the same time in Glasgow. She is very careful, however, not to overemphasize the local dimension in the construction of this local political world, and goes on to show how local circumstances in the two cities were shaped in different ways by attitudes towards questions of national identity – a dialectical relationship between the local and the national which produced different 'systems of beliefs' in the two cities which were reflected in their very different political construction:

The construction of those local states was ... on the basis of the particular economic and social circumstances of those cities, including their particular labour market and housing stock. However, it would be quite wrong to interpret the history of relations between Irish groups and others in these cities as if those relations were born directly out of the job or housing markets.

The beliefs of workers in Glasgow and Liverpool cannot be reduced to their market situation or to some abstract 'colonialism'. The different beliefs of the Protestant majorities about the Irish arose out of their entire way of seeing the world. And this world view was a belief system that was constructed in the political and social circumstances of their particular towns over a fifty-year period. The skilled men of Glasgow were, by and large, Liberals. Their Liberalism held within it quite different attitudes to the national state from those of the Conservatism of Liverpool. In Glasgow, Protestant working men did not necessarily identify with the entire nation state; like Gladstone they objected to the 'classes' of the landed aristocrary and the Established Church. In Liverpool, on the other hand, the question of national identity overwhelmed other questions in the beliefs of working men, both those of the 'majority' and those of the 'minority'. Thus the Irish nationalist movement that developed in Liverpool was much more Irish and Catholic than the one that developed in Glasgow. It was in this way that the ethnic community of Liverpool was politically constructed. It did not arise automatically from the existence of large numbers of Irish in Liverpool, nor did it arise automatically from the housing and labour market. In both Glasgow and Liverpool relationships between the Irish-Catholic and the Protestant were, therefore, negotiated and constructed within political contexts determined largely by the strength of identity with the nation and of the social organizations that reinforced or challenged nationalist beliefs.

(Smith, 1986, p. 202)

Just as this interplay between local and national contexts and relationships helped in the construction of Liverpool's Conservative local state, so too was a similar interplay important in its dismantling. At local level, the breaking up of the geography of ethnic segregation as a result of rehousing people from both sides of the sectarian divide to the peripheral council estates, in the inter-war years and especially in the 1950s and 1960s, had a powerful effect in minimizing the religious tension and conflict that had been sustained by the ethnically segregated and juxtaposed inner-city districts (Davies, 1980). In terms of questions of national identity, the establishment of the Irish Free State in 1922 reduced the importance of the 'Irish Question'. This is not to argue that the question of religion has played no part in the reconstruction of the local state (the local Labour Party, for example, was split over the question of the building of the Roman Catholic Cathedral and, more recently, a Militant-led council came into conflict with an inner-city housing cooperative in which religion had provided an important source of solidarity), but its influence has been greatly reduced. And there has been no resurgence of the sectarian violence of the kind that was endemic in the life of the town in the latter part of the nineteenth century and the early part of the current one.

2.3.3 Musical connections

If the city is known for its history of political struggles and social unrest, it is also known for its cultural history and, in particular, its contributions to music. Again, I would argue, this local world of music cannot be understood outside of the context of the global interconnections discussed in the previous section. Perhaps one of the most obvious links can be traced through the Irish diaspora. We have already seen how the latter was important in the constitution of local politics. The 'Irishness' of the town can also be seen in its music. Reading B is an extract from Kevin McManus's study of Irish music in Liverpool.

Activity 5 Read Reading B, 'Céilís, jigs and ballads: Irish music in Liverpool', and think about the significance for understanding 'local worlds' of the following:

o The way in which Irish traditional music has developed in a constant movement between the 'home country' and distant 'local worlds' created by migrants.

o The importance of ethnic identity and 'roots': apart from the obvious reasons, why is it important for Liverpudlians of Irish descent to know the gaelic words for men's and women's toilets?

o The importance of connections between places – even if, as in the Ireland jaunt of the Liverpool Céilí Band described in the extract, you may not always leave on time.

o The way in which new generations take traditional music and reshape it in the light of their own cultural experiences and understanding, making it '... contemporary in form and culture, yet ... culturally familiar also'.

o The idea that there is not only Irishness in Liverpool but also Liverpool in its Irishness.

Of course, the Irish influence that Kevin McManus was exploring in Reading B came from that first link in the connection between Ireland, Liverpool and America. It is also possible to trace two-way musical influences in the second link in that journey – in the local development of country-and-western music. As the title of Reading C acknowledges, another title that Liverpool can lay claim to is that of 'Nashville of the North', because of its leading role in the development of country-and-western music in Britain. In the extract, Kevin McManus discusses the reasons why a band with the name the 'Blue Mountain Boys' came from a city which has at best a view of the Clwydian Range in North Wales – and then only on a clear day and from a relatively small number of vantage points.

Activity 6 Read Reading C, '"Nashville of the North": country music in Liverpool', by Kevin McManus.

o What does it tell us about the role of 'global connections' in constituting 'local worlds'?

o What were the roots of country-and-western? What mixes of what worlds?

o Note the different types of 'global connections' represented by the 'Cunard Yanks' and the Burtonwood airbase.

o Just how 'local' are Liverpool's country-and-western bands?

Reading C referred to another cultural phenomenon for which Liverpool is more internationally renowned – 'Merseybeat'. The question that is important here, of course, is to what extent was this musical phenomenon a *Mersey*beat (or the so-called 'Liverpool Sound' with which recording companies became besotted in the 1960s)? The answer, I would argue, is that it was neither a purely local nor a simply global phenomenon – it was, in the terminology of cultural anthropology, a classic example of *hybridity*. It was a case of local

cultural hybridity

musicians taking the sounds from America – the sounds of both the black and Irish diasporas (constituted chiefly and respectively through rhythm and blues and county-and-western music) – and adapting them and reinterpreting them with a local 'feel'. No group of local musicians did that with more world-changing effect than the Beatles. Feeding into that sound were the American records brought back to the port by the 'Cunard Yanks', and the influences of both film (especially films with Bill Haley and, later, Elvis Presley in them) and radio (with stations like Radio Luxembourg broadcasting popular music night and day).

It is a well known tale that the two main songwriters in the group met at a local fête where John Lennon, who had been playing in his 'skiffle group' the Quarry Men, was introduced, in a memorably inebriated state, to Paul McCartney. Skiffle groups like Liverpool's Quarry Men formed an important stage in the development of British popular music (Denselow, 1989). They were largely inspired by a British artist, Lonnie Donegan, who developed a commercialized and, importantly, with its three-chord style, relatively easy to play version of early country blues and 'folk' music including the songs, for example, of Woody Guthrie and Huddie 'Leadbelly' Ledbetter. This music, already a hybridized version of the original American songs, was further hybridized by the British groups who struggled to play it. And none, by all accounts, struggled more than the Quarry Men. Their own set list of songs, however, does reveal their own version of hybridity: including Leadbelly's 'Rock Island Line' (in its Lonnie Donegan-ized form), Chas McDevitt and Nancy Whiskey's 'Freight Train', Johnny Duncan's 'Last Train to San Fernando', and – a local input – 'Maggie May', an old sailors' song about a Liverpool woman of some notoriety (Coleman, 1984).

John Lennon's introduction to Paul McCartney led, of course, to the production of a body of original music which changed the whole course of popular music, and popular culture more widely – on a global scale. The Beatles took music that had itself been shaped by the global interconnections

The Beatles in Liverpool's docklands in 1962, around the time of their first journeys to London to make the records that were to change the course of popular music across the world

in which the city had been important and then filtered it through their own 'local world' (in some cases actually using local places – 'Penny Lane', 'Strawberry Fields' – for inspiration and reference points). The results were then fed back into the global. Their musical influences are revealed in the songs that they chose to 'cover' on their recordings, but the Beatles themselves were always willing to acknowledge their musical debts. Box 2.8 contains some of John Lennon's thoughts on these debts, recognizing the importance of both black rhythm and blues and white country-and-western influences and revealing, in the process, both a very strong geographical imagination and a rather shaky understanding of the 'triangular trade'.

Box 2.8 John Lennon on musical influences and living in Liverpool

'When I started Rock and Roll itself was a basic revolution to people of my age and situation. We needed something loud and clear to break through all the unfeeling and repression that had been coming down on us kids. We were a bit conscious to begin with of being imitation Americans. But we delved into music and found that it was half white Country-and-Western and half black Rhythm and Blues. Most of the songs came from Europe and Africa and now they were coming back to us. ... It was a sort of cultural exchange.'

Source: John Lennon, quoted in Miles, 1980, p. 97

'Q. What did being from Liverpool have to do with your art?

A. It's the second biggest port in England. The north is where the money was made in the 1800s; that was where all the brass and the heavy people were, and that's where the despised people were. We were the ones who were looked down upon as animals by the southerners, the Londoners. In the States, the Northerners think that down South, people are pigs, and the people in New York think West Coast is hick. So we were Hicksville.

Liverpool is a very poor city and tough. But people have a sense of humour because they are in so much pain. So they are always cracking jokes, and they are very witty. It's an Irish place, too; it is where the Irish came when they ran out of potatoes, and it's where black people were left or worked as slaves or whatever.

It is cosmopolitan, and it's where the sailors would come home with blues records from America. Liverpool has the biggest country and western following in England besides London – always besides London because there is more of it there.

I heard country and western music in Liverpool before I heard rock and roll. The people take their country and western music very seriously. I remember the first guitar I ever saw. It belonged to a guy in a cowboy suit and a cowboy hat and a big dobro. They were real cowboys and they took it seriously. There were cowboys long before there was rock and roll.'

Source: John Lennon, quoted in Wenner, 1987, p. 102

Thinking about all these global connections linked to the Black and Irish diasporas and the whole history of British colonial development and Empire, there has to be both a certain irony and also a certain historical correctness in the Labour Government's decision in 1965 to make the Beatles Members of the Order of the British Empire. Just think of all those colonial and 'Empire' connections (from the rhythm and blues of the black diaspora and the country-and-western music shaped by the Irish diaspora to George Harrison's incorporation of Indian sitar music into the Beatles' 'sound').

2.3.4   Trading places: Liverpool and Rotterdam

In section 2.2.3, it was suggested that the relationship between Liverpool and
Rotterdam needs to be seen in the broader processes of *uneven development* in
which Liverpool's economic decline has mirrored Rotterdam's growth: a
former 'gateway to Empire' struggling against a new 'gateway to Europe'. The
prevailing geography of uneven development, of course, contains other local
worlds whose development will affect that of Liverpool. The point I want to
make here is the simple one that as Rotterdam, and other places similarly
favoured in the current phase of global economic and political restructuring,
move closer to the 'centre' of the economic map so to speak, Liverpool and
places similarly disfavoured are pushed to the margins. Local worlds involved
in this reshaping of the global mosaic of uneven development are thus
presented with an ongoing 'identity crisis' as they come to terms with their
new situation, and their new 'place'. In the final section of the chapter, I
want to explore some of the ways in which Liverpool has adjusted to its
relocation on the global economic and political map.

uneven development

Summary of section 2.3

o   The representation of a place is often structured around opposition
    to others (in Liverpool's case, for example, in opposition to
    Manchester over the port and to national opinion over the
    abolition of slavery).

o   The representation of a place can be gendered (e.g. the masculinity
    of historical representations of Liverpool), and can similarly be
    affected by issues of race and ethnicity (e.g. the controversy over
    the town's representation of its participation in the slave trade).

o   Social and spatial segregation helps to produce 'local worlds' within
    'local worlds' (e.g. social-spatial segregation on the grounds of race
    and religion; the importance of 'territoriality'). This social and
    spatial segregation can produce a 'localism' in which sharp
    distinctions are drawn between 'insiders' and 'outsiders', which can
    in turn have important effects on the development of the 'local
    world' as a whole (e.g. religious segregation helping to shape local
    politics).

o   Even in the development of 'local worlds' within 'local worlds',
    wider factors are important (e.g. the importance of national
    political identities in local political formation).

o   The hybrid nature of cultural exchange reinforces the point that it
    is impossible to separate the local from the global (e.g. the
    development of Irish music and country-and-western music in
    Liverpool; the hybridity of 'Merseybeat').

o   Economic links between places are constructed and reconstructed
    in a process of uneven development in which there are winners and
    losers and in which the issues of the identification with and
    representation of places are constantly presenting themselves.

2.4 Local worlds, global connections and uneven development

2.4.1 Local worlds, uneven development and crises of identity

Figure 2.6 gives one indication of the reversal in Liverpool's economic fortunes. It charts the phenomenal growth of the city during the eighteenth century and the equally phenomenal decline of the last sixty years or so. The labelling of the horizontal axis of the graph is an attempt to underline the point that, to understand this trajectory of growth, it is necessary to understand the town's global interconnections, its changing historical global economic and political 'place'. Reading along the axis we can see how growth accelerated with Britain's colonial 'adventures', the Atlantic trade, European industrialization and the formation of an international division of labour based on unequal trading relationships between 'core' and 'periphery'. The previous two sections give some idea of the way in which Liverpool was reconstituted and represented in this developing web of global interconnections. Figure 2.6 also shows how Liverpool's recent decline is similarly set within a new global economic and political context and a newly emerging web of global relationships: the evolution of a new international division of labour (based on the globalization of production, involving the emergence of newly industrializing countries, and dominated by the activities of multinational corporations), and the making of a 'New Europe'. And we saw in section 2.2.3 how Rotterdam, for example, is much better 'placed' in this 'New Europe' than is Liverpool.

In section 2.3.4, I hinted at the way in which 'local worlds' experiencing changing economic fortunes perhaps linked to changes in their global interconnections may undergo what can be described as 'identity crises'. Indeed, it could be argued that it is precisely when people in places feel themselves threatened by developments seemingly outside their control that the issues of identification with place and representation of place become more urgent.

Liverpool's recent history certainly provides a number of examples of this kind of identity crisis. The much publicized confrontation between the city's ruling Labour administration and Conservative central government in the mid-1980s took place against the backcloth of just such a crisis. Economic decline, outmigration from an increasingly proletarianized city, and popular discontent with the policies of both local and national government paved the way in 1983 for the election of a local Labour administration controlled by a far-left 'Militant' faction. Elected in 1983 with 46 per cent of the vote (the highest vote in the history of the local Labour Party), it decided to fund its programme with a deficit budget which quickly brought it into conflict with a Conservative central government dedicated to limiting the autonomy of local government. It was a risky strategy given the prevailing balance of political forces, and it eventually failed, but what stood out was the way in which the confrontation with central government mobilized local political support, not so much around the Militant council but more around the city. John Bohanna, a shop steward at a local car factory, nicely captured the mood of the times: ' "It's our city that's under attack", that's how most people I talked to saw it … Every Scouser loves Scouseland, they regard it as *their* city. That's what was at stake: our city, not the Labour Party, not Militant' (quoted in Wainwright, 1987, p. 130).

Notice the way in which local feelings that the city was under attack encouraged identification with the city and acceptance of a particular representation of it – that of the Militant council administration – against the representation of a perceived 'outsider', an unsympathetic central government.

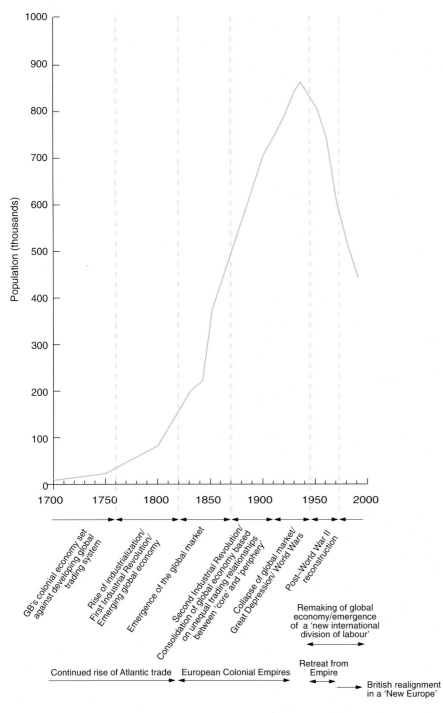

Figure 2.6 *Liverpool's population in global economic and political context*

Another example was provided by the media coverage of the horrific murder of a child in the city by two young children. The scale of the expressions of sympathy for the family of the victim through entries in the obituary columns of the local press (whole editions were virtually devoted to them) was used by one national newspaper to mount an attack on what it perceived as 'Self-pity City'. This provoked an almost despairing sense of local outrage that was aired on local radio and television and in the local and national press. In this public self-reflection, the response that 'outsiders' had interpreted as 'self-pitying' was seen by 'insiders' as a genuine communal expression of grief and solidarity with the bereaved – the response not of some kind of 'dysfunctional city' but rather of a 'caring' and 'compassionate city'. Once again the people of the city were being forced to reassess their views of the place in which they lived and, by extension, their views of themselves and their relationships with each other in that place. The attack on 'Liverpool' was an attack on them.

Decline and the perceived economic and political marginalization of the city have also led to an intensification of the ever-present rivalry with Manchester. The issue is again about global connections, only this time it is about connections by air rather than by sea.

Liverpool's airport is completely overshadowed by its Manchester counterpart – with just three international destinations and no scheduled passenger flight to Heathrow in London (compared with Manchester Airport's sixty international destinations and regular London 'shuttle flight'). Developing Liverpool's airport is seen by local politicians as essential for reconnecting the city to national and global networks. The problem that this strategy faces, however, is the current proposal by Manchester Airport to expand its facilities. The historical rivalry between the two cities has been revived in what one national newspaper described as a 'political dogfight in the North'. It is, of course, a dogfight that is being staged in a context of dramatically changed relationships between the two towns. As Eric Williams argued in relation to a different time: 'In the age of mercantilism Manchester was Liverpool's hinterland, in the age of *laissez faire* Liverpool was Manchester's suburb' (1944, p. 162). In many ways the latter relationship still holds – and representations of the town continue to be shaped by these relationships of interconnection.

It should be clear from the discussion so far that how places are represented is not solely the preserve of the people living in them – the representation of places is shaped by external as well as internal relationships. Liverpool has certainly received more than its fair share of 'outsider' attention. What stands out is the way in which these 'outsider' views have been mediated and reinterpreted by 'insiders'. One increasingly visible way in which this occurs is in the form of 'place marketing' initiatives by local development agencies. When you put the two together (as Figure 2.7 attempts to do), you are left with a kind of discordant, schizophrenic 'imagined place', a cacophony of confusing messages. In Liverpool's case, it appears to be all 'doom and gloom' from outside (if you look carefully at Figure 2.7 you will see the 'Self-pity City' accusation) and all 'boom' from the local economic development lobby (itself often a 'colonial arm' of central government). Somewhere in the middle of all this are the residents of the city – and the different groups that these comprise – attempting to make sense of a 'real' local world that provides the setting for, in Geertz's words, '… the diversity of the ways human beings construct their lives in the act of leading them' (1993, p. 16).

Reborn city of vision and values

Liverpool is beginning to thrive again. **Ronald Faux** presents a two-page report

Symbol of dignity in a city that has suffered: St George's Hall, regarded by the Prince of Wales as one of the greatest building

Famous docks back on stream

Record tonnages and profits

Panorama of growing prosperity

Mersey beats the drum about region's revival

Prediction Trevor Furlong

It's boom-time NOW for Liverpool hotels

By Diana Pulson

Mersey turns the tide

BY CORINNE SIMCOCK

Liverpool steps up to blow its own trumpet

Gary Mead reports on moves to woo US investors

Walking tall with success again

City's lifeblood is draining away

LIVING IN THE GARB AGE

Port at sea on a rising tide of debt

Cultural profile LIVERPOOL

Proud city down in the dumps

Can rubbish-strewn Liverpool clean up its act, asks **Michael Parkinson**

en prepare to vote today

When the Walton by-election circus leaves town, Liverpool will be left to clear up the mess. **Colin Brown** and **Jonathan Foster** report

SELF-PITY CITY

THE CITY THAT BRITAIN FAILED

'No end in sight to Liverpool's despair'

A city in decline

Like blacks in the United States, Liverpudlians are now on the proscribed list. You publicly find fault with them at your peril

Welcome to Utopia in Liverpool. Once they must queue to live here. Now they must survive in a decaying haunt of drug addicts and criminals. Report by Peter Beaumont Photographs by Neil Libbert

No money, no jobs,

Figure 2.7 Two tales of a city

The newspaper article reproduced below shows that place marketing continues in Liverpool. And so does that predisposition to represent the city in opposition to other places. This time the proposed opponent is an apparently much offended Surbiton.

Liverpool, city with an image problem, seeks slick slogan

David Ward on the struggle to find right words without offending Surbiton

Liverpool wants to change its image. Or, more correctly, it wants London-based reporters to change their image of the city's image.

Away with gloom, doom, grot and misery. In with the truth about Liverpool in 1994. 'Did you know that there is more lobster bisque sold in Marks and Spencer's in Liverpool than in their Knightsbridge store?' asked Peter Davies, head of the city's public relations department.

When the city fathers pondered how to persuade those beyond the Mersey to confront reality, Mr Davies suggested a slogan: 'Liverpool – it isn't Surbiton'.

Surbiton went puce. 'This is just outrageous,' said the London suburb's Liberal Democrat councillor Jen Tankard. 'Surbiton is a greener, safer, cleaner environment than Liverpool. Pollution is dreadful there and crime is far higher.'

Mr Davies was shocked. Simple statement of truth, no value judgements, he insisted, after saying a few things about yuppies, mobile phones and BMWs. 'We haven't insulted them. There must be a lot of insecurity in Surbiton. Are people ashamed about living there? I expect they are making Molotov cocktails as we speak.'

Liverpool plans to consult the people on its image. 'Other places ask only the opinion of the great and the good,' said Mr Davies. 'We are talking to focus groups which will include the unemployed, school children and the black community as well as business people and local worthies.'

The city has hired a PR firm for £25,000 to sift through the ideas that emerge.

Yesterday the Guardian attempted – for no payment whatsoever – to collect slogan ideas.

The Royal Liverpool Philharmonic recalled that Jung had called the city The Pool of Life and settled for that.

The Beatle Story museum at Albert Dock tried for echoes of John Lennon with 'Liverpool – more than you'd imagine'.

North-west Tonight, the BBC's regional television news magazine, came up with 'Feel the pride, feel the passion'.

But what of Liverpool's eloquent writers? Alan Bleasdale (Boys From The Blackstuff and GBH) said: 'I thought about it for 30 seconds and couldn't think of anything that wouldn't offend the moral majority.'

No luck there; nor with Willy Russell (Educating Rita and Blood Brothers): 'If I could think of anything, I'd be copy-righting it now – I wouldn't be sitting here writing a bloody novel. Have you tried Roger McGough?'

Mr McGough, now in exile in London, was prolific. 'How about "Liverpool – there's no getting away from it"? Or "Liverpool – the heart of the nation" or "Liverpool – a mind of its own" or "Liverpool – no less" or "Liverpool – out on its own" or "Liverpool – it's another world".'

The best effort came from the collective deconstructionist mind of the staff of Museums and Galleries on Merseyside: 'Liverpool – too good for slogans.'

Beat that, Surbiton.

Source: *The Guardian*, 21 May 1994

Activity 7 Compare the competing 'images' of the city in Figure 2.7. Why do you think that there is such a sharp contrast in the representation of the same place? Who is doing the imagining? Is one image more 'real' than another?

Read the newspaper extract opposite and think about the issues surrounding 'place marketing'. Image making for whom? Image making by whom? Whose place is being represented? What are the implications of places being 'sold' in competition with other places?

2.4.2   Reconnecting local worlds?

As the competing messages in Figure 2.7 indicate, 'place marketing' in places like Liverpool produces a kind of schizophrenia among local politicians and local government officers and agencies involved in local economic development. On the one hand, they are attempting to present positive images to outside investors (on the lines of the 'reborn city of vision and values' in Figure 2.7) while, on the other hand, also being engaged in presenting negative images to secure assistance from national and supranational government (on the lines of the 'proud city down in the dumps' in Figure 2.7).

In Liverpool's case, its most recent involvement in this form of negative place marketing has been particularly successful. After active local lobbying it was recognized, along with the four other local authority districts which together with the city make up Merseyside, as part of an 'Objective 1' region eligible for the highest levels of assistance under the European Union's Structural Funds. 'Objective 1' regions are officially defined as 'lagging regions' with output per head of population at levels three-quarters or less of the European Union average. Liverpool is thus very firmly located at the disadvantaged core of what is the first industrialized region within the European Union to be given the official status of a 'lagging region'. Just think for a moment about the imagery of that description. In a competitive global economic race some regions and places are falling behind others, like runners or cyclists being separated and distanced from the leading pack.

The assistance to be provided – with 'matching' national and local funds something like £1.2 billion over a five-year period – is designed somehow to reconnect the region into the European and global economy, and specifically to close the gap in output levels between the region and the European average. The agreed plan talks about 'convergence', and running throughout it, alongside measures designed to assist local industries and local people, are measures aimed at reconnecting the region with other places – through airport and seaport development and through telecommunications links.

In addition to somewhat traditional policies for the support of industry, the plan also distinguishes what it calls 'action for the people of Merseyside' through 'pathways to integration, a better training system, community development and a better quality of life'. The 'pathways to integration' are specifically aimed at individuals and groups 'excluded' from participating in the local economy – such as young people with little education or training, the long-term unemployed, and women experiencing discrimination in the labour market and/or burdened with caring responsibilities. And the plan recognizes that there are areas within the region in which these groups are particularly concentrated. The aim of this part of the plan is to encourage the coordination and mobilization of the whole panoply of local educational and training provision (public, private and voluntary) to minimize the problems of 'exclusion' experienced by these groups. It also serves as both a recognition and reminder of the fact that 'lagging regions', 'disconnected places' mean economic and *social exclusion* – exclusion from the mainstream of economic and social life for individuals and groups of people living within them.

social exclusion

This is not the place to go into the merits or otherwise of the Objective 1 plan. For the purposes of this chapter, however, what the plan does do is to bring into sharp focus the issues that face 'local worlds' whose economic activities have become disconnected from the mainstream global economy with all that that implies for local standards of living, the local social fabric and so on. Can they be reconnected? Will there always be some places that succeed in economic terms at the expense of others? Is it places that are 'disconnected' or people who are 'excluded'? If this chapter has achieved anything, I would hope that it would have convinced you that any attempt to begin to answer questions such as these stretches our geographical imaginations.

Summary of section 2.4

o The response of people who feel threatened by 'outside' forces and images of the places in which they live may be to heighten their sense of identification with those places – an attack on place is often perceived by the people living there as an attack on themselves.

o How we represent places is shaped by both internal and external relationships, and there can be conflicting 'images' of the same place.

o 'Place marketing' may have to promote negative as well as positive messages (to secure government intervention).

o Behind the imagery of 'lagging regions' and 'disconnected places' are individuals and groups of people experiencing economic and social exclusion.

References

AYERS, P. (1990) *The Liverpool Docklands: Life and Work in Athol Street*, University of Liverpool, Dockland History Project.

BELCHEM, J. (1992) 'Liverpool in the year of revolution: the political and associational culture of the Irish immigrant community in 1848', in Belchem, J. (ed.) *Popular Politics, Riot and Labour: Essays in Liverpool History, 1790–1940*, Liverpool, Liverpool University Press.

BOHSTEDT, J. (1992) 'More than one working class: Protestant and Catholic riots in Edwardian Liverpool', in Belchem, J. (ed.) *Popular Politics, Riot and Labour: Essays in Liverpool History, 1790–1940*, Liverpool, Liverpool University Press.

CAMERON, G. and CROOKE, S. (1992) *Liverpool – Capital of the Slave Trade*, Liverpool, Picton Press.

COLEMAN, R. (1984) *John Lennon*, London, Futura.

COLLEY, L. (1992) *Britons: Forging the Nation 1707–1837*, London, Pimlico.

DAVIES, P.N. (1973) *The Trade Makers: Elder Dempster in West Africa, 1852–1972*, London, Allen and Unwin.

DAVIES, R.S.W. (1980) 'The Liverpool Labour Party and the Liverpool working class, 1900–1939', *North West Labour History Society Bulletin*, 6, Liverpool.

DAVIS, G. (1991) *The Irish in Britain 1815–1914*, Dublin, Gill and Macmillan Ltd.

DE VRIES, J. (1984) *European Urbanization 1500–1800*, London, Methuen.

DENSELOW, R. (1989) *When the Music's Over: The Story of Political Pop*, London, Faber and Faber.

DICKEY SAM (1884) *Liverpool and Slavery: An Historical Account of the Liverpool-African Slave Trade*, Liverpool, A. Bowker & Son. Reprint published 1985, Liverpool, Scouse Press.

DOYLE, W. (1992) *The Old European Order 1660–1800*, Oxford, Oxford University Press.

ELTIS, D. (1987) *Economic Growth and the Ending of the Transatlantic Slave Trade*, Oxford, Oxford University Press.

FRYER, P. (1984) *Staying Power: The History of Black People in Britain*, London, Pluto Press.

GALLAGHER, T. (1985) 'A tale of two cities: communal strife in Glasgow and Liverpool before 1914', in Swift, R. and Gilley, S. (eds) *The Irish in the Victorian City*, Beckenham, Croom Helm Ltd.

GEERTZ, C. (1993) *Local Knowledge*, London, Fontana Press.

GILROY, P. (1993) *Small Acts: Thoughts on the Politics of Black Cultures*, London, Serpent's Tail.

GILROY, P. (1994) *The Black Atlantic*, London, Verso.

GRANT, L. (1987) *Women Workers and the Sexual Division of Labour: Liverpool 1890–1939*, unpublished Ph.D. thesis, University of Liverpool.

HAYUTH, Y. and HILLING, D. (1992) 'Technological change and seaport development', in Hoyle, B.S. and Pinder, D.A. (eds) *European Port Cities in Transition*, London, Belhaven Press.

HOPKINS, A.G. (1973) *An Economic History of West Africa*, Harlow, Longman.

HYDE, F.E. (1971) *Liverpool and the Mersey: An Economic History of a Port, 1700–1970*, Newton Abbot, David and Charles.

KARRAS, A.L. and McNEILL, J.R. (eds) (1992) *Atlantic American Societies from Columbus through Abolition, 1492–1888*, London, Routledge.

KNOX, P. and AGNEW, J. (1994) *The Geography of the World Economy: An Introduction to Economic Geography* (2nd edn), London, Edward Arnold.

LANE, T. (1987) *Liverpool: Gateway of Empire*, London, Lawrence and Wishart.

LAWTON, R. and POOLEY, C. (1992) *Britain 1740–1950: An Historical Geography*, London, Edward Arnold.

LIVERPOOL CITY COUNCIL (1930) *The City of Liverpool Official Handbook*, Liverpool, Liverpool City Council.

LIVERPOOL CITY COUNCIL (1993) *1991 Census: Key Statistics Liverpool Wards 1971/81/91*, Liverpool, Liverpool City Council.

MANNING, P. (1992) 'Tragedy and sacrifice in the history of slavery', in Karras, A.L. and McNeill, J.R. (eds) (1992).

MARRINER, S. (1982) *The Economic and Social Development of Merseyside*, London, Croom Helm.

MASSEY, D. (1994) *Space, Place and Gender*, Minneapolis, University of Minnesota Press.

McMANUS, K. (1994a) *Céilís, Jigs and Ballads: Irish Music in Liverpool*, Liverpool, Institute of Popular Music, University of Liverpool.

McMANUS, K. (1994b) '*Nashville of the North': Country Music in Liverpool*, Liverpool, Institute of Popular Music, University of Liverpool.

MILES (1980) *John Lennon In His Own Words*, London, Omnibus Press.

MILLER, K.A. (1985) *Emigrants and Exiles: Ireland and the Irish Exodus to North America*, New York, Oxford University Press.

MOUNTFIELD, S. (1965) *Western Gateway: A History of the Mersey Docks and Harbour Board*, Liverpool, Liverpool University Press.

MUIR, J.R.B. (1907) *A History of Liverpool*, London, Williams and Norgate (for University of Liverpool Press).

MUSGROVE, F. (1990) *The North of England: A History from Roman Times to the Present*, Oxford, Blackwell.

NATIONAL GEOGRAPHIC SOCIETY (1988) *Historical Atlas of the United States*, Washington DC, National Geographic Society.

NEAL, F. (1988) *Sectarian Violence: The Liverpool Experience, 1819–1914: An Aspect of Anglo-Irish History*, Manchester, Manchester University Press.

PARKINSON, C.N. (1952) *The Rise of the Port of Liverpool*, Liverpool, Liverpool University Press.

POLLOCK, E.E. (1981) 'Free ports, free trade zones, export processing zones and economic development', in Hoyle, B.S. and Pinder, D.A. (eds) *Cityport Industrialization and Regional Development: Spatial Analysis and Planning Strategies*, Oxford, Pergamon Press.

POSTMA, J.M. (1990) *The Dutch in the Atlantic Slave Trade 1600–1815*, Cambridge, Cambridge University Press.

POTTS, L. (1990) *The World Labour Market: A History of Migration*, London, Zed Books.

SMITH, J. (1984) 'Labour tradition in Glasgow and Liverpool', *History Workshop*, 17, Spring, pp. 32–56.

SMITH, J. (1986) 'Class, skill and sectarianism in Glasgow and Liverpool, 1880–1914', in Morris, R.J. (ed.) *Class, Power and Social Structure in British Nineteenth Century Towns*, Leicester, Leicester University Press.

TAPLIN, E. (1986) *The Dockers' Union: A Study of the National Union of Dock Labourers, 1889–1922*, Leicester, Leicester University Press.

UNSWORTH, B. (1992) *Sacred Hunger*, Harmondsworth, Penguin Books.

VAN HELMOND, M. and PALMER, D. (1991) *Staying Power: Black Presence in Liverpool*, Liverpool, National Museum and Galleries on Merseyside.

WAINWRIGHT, H. (1987) *Labour: A Tale of Two Parties*, London, The Hogarth Press.

WALLER, P.J. (1981) *Democracy and Sectarianism: A Political and Social History of Liverpool 1868–1939*, Liverpool, Liverpool University Press.

WENNER, J. (ed.) (1987) *20 Years of Rolling Stone: What a Long, Strange Trip It's Been*, London, Ebury Press.

WILLIAMS, E. (1944) *Capitalism and Slavery*, London, André Deutsch.

WILLIAMS, E. (1970) *From Columbus to Castro: The History of the Caribbean 1492–1969*, London, André Deutsch.

WILLIAMS, G. (1897) *History of the Liverpool Privateers and Letters of Marque with an Account of the Liverpool Slave Trade*, London and Liverpool, William Heinemann.

WOLF, E.R. (1982) *Europe and the People Without History*, Berkeley and Los Angeles, University of California Press.

Reading A: *Linda Grant, 'Women workers and the sexual division of labour: Liverpool 1890–1939'*

[…] In Liverpool, one central aspect of local economic conditions which had a bearing on women's experience as workers and mothers was the casual recruitment of local male workers.

The consequences of casualism identified in this study as having a crucial bearing on women's relationship to waged work and their location within the occupational structure are poverty, the inability of thousands of local working-class families to escape the slum housing centred on the dockside areas, and a workplace culture amongst the dock workforce that sharpened a masculine consciousness which drew clear distinctions between the spheres of men's and women's economic activity.

Poverty and a hand-to-mouth existence structured countless thousands of lives in Liverpool during the period of this study. And the extremely poor housing in the dockland areas left many families living in miserable, health-threatening conditions. This poor quality of life was experienced most acutely by women, since they shouldered burdens not encountered by men. Pregnancy, childbearing, childcare and the struggle to make ends meet placed a constant, debilitating strain on women's health. Lack of funds meant poor nourishment, poor household equipment and no medical care for women. High infant mortality rates and widespread maternal morbidity reflected this.

Despite the strains imposed on women in the home, however, few women were able to choose not to seek waged work. The irregular earnings of men created households in which women's wages were vital to family survival. But women entered a severely restricted labour market, unable to employ all those women who sought work. The consequence of this for the woman worker was that her conditions of employment were invariably wretched. Low pay, long hours of work, insanitary working conditions, oppressive supervision, insecurity of employment and irregular working were the characteristic features of women's daily experiences at their workplaces. Those factors which typically defined women's working lives in Britain were exaggerated and intensified in the context of an - inflated supply of female labour. All the oppressive and exploitative practices which confronted women workers generally came into sharp focus. Thus, even in those industries which relied on skilled, experienced women workers, such as the tobacco industry, employment conditions were characteristically poor. In many households, of course, there were no male workers. But the low level of female wages prevalent locally left many widows and single women, women on whom others were often dependent, barely surviving on the margins of poverty and periodically forced to depend on the Parish and the workhouse.

The circumstances created by the intermittent and fluctuating earnings of men, combined with a limited market for female labour, intensified the characteristic features of the sexual division of labour in Britain whereby women were heavily concentrated in the personal service industry. In Liverpool, thousands of women in each generation were paid at the very lowest wage levels as step cleaners, office cleaners, washerwomen, laundry workers, shop cleaners, chambermaids, domestic servants, charwomen, waitresses and cleaners on board ship. Liverpool was a city in which the sexual division of labour came into the sharpest relief.

The significance of the personal service industry within the Liverpool economy has been neglected in the literature concerned with the city's history. But this was a phenomenon of immense importance. For thousands of women,

their horizons of employment did not extent beyond domestic work. Moreover, it could be argued, the size of this industry made it as characteristic of the Liverpool economy as work in and around the port. Women's work, however, has little resonance within our images and understanding of a particular community primarily because much of this work is hidden. The office is cleaned in the early hours before the office worker arrives, the ship is cleaned whilst the seafarer is on shore leave, women wash and clean in their own homes and in other people's homes, isolated one from another and invisible as workers. It is only when we reflect on the size of this section of the workforce and the importance of women's earnings to households of underemployed workers, that its significance becomes apparent. The sheer number of female resident domestic servants in the city – 20,000 and more each year – underlines this, but this workforce has been consistently overlooked in the analysis of Liverpool's past. The neglect of women's history in the city amounts to an ignorance of the unique working relationships in which a significant section of the working class were involved. Furthermore, we overlook the important fact that the nature and conditions of women's work in this period of Liverpool's history were as illustrative of the limitations of the local economy as was the surplus of dockers. The impact of the city's economic dependence on trade defined women's lives as much as men's lives.

I have argued that the culture and consciousness generated amongst the male dock workforce stressed and applauded the demonstration of skills and abilities inextricably linked with masculinity in our society. Implicit within this culture was the delineation of femininity and a distinct female world. An entrenched relationship between gender and occupation was partly sustained by people's very sense of themselves as male and female. The boundaries of the female labour market were supported by a consciousness which defined the essence of masculinity and femininity.

[...] One major focus of political representation and trade unionism in

Liverpool was the port and its workforce. Dockers were drawn into the political arena by virtue of the importance of the port to the local and national economy [...] Thus the campaigns and recruitment programmes of the trade union movement found a central focus amongst dock workers. One can speculate that on this basis dockers had the potential to command political attention and exercise the rights of citizenship to an extent denied to women. The involvement of men in the struggles, campaigns and committees of the trade unions was a basis for their incorporation into the political life of the city as a whole. Women, outside of this primary economic activity of the city, tended to be marginalized not only economically but also politically. The majority of women lacked trade union representation and, as a result, were less involved as citizens. Women were placed outside of those issues and interests which strongly influenced the local political agenda. Women's concerns as citizens and workers were defined as of secondary importance to those of men by virtue of the prevailing ideologies which contrasted the status and economic contribution of men and women. But local conditions were inextricably interconnected with these ideologies of gender division, reinforcing the tendency to exclude women from the political arena. [...]

This study has traced the fortunes of women workers in a number of local industries which employed large numbers of women in the period under review. A number of themes have emerged in this analysis. First [...] was the poverty and abysmal working conditions which typically confronted female workers in Liverpool. A second theme is the way in which industrial restructuring and increasing capital investment in a number of manufacturing industries tended to encourage the transfer of women out of work formally recognized as skilled into semi-skilled and unskilled processes. Gradually, but consistently, changes in the labour process annihilated the 'skilled woman worker'. The effects of this were significant for local women workers. Materially women were denied

the prospect of relatively well-paid work. In this sense, the pre-existing characteristics of the sexual division of labour were progressively more sharply drawn. There were also more general ideological consequences of the increasing obsolescence of certain skills held by women. The equation skill/women became gradually more tenuous, less real. The loss in skill status experienced by specific groups of women workers reinforced the tendency to categorize all women's work as unskilled [...] Thus [...] there was a tendency for the objective skills retained by women to be degraded. The adverse consequences of the sexual division of labour for local women workers were thus consistently confirmed, materially and ideologically.

Closely related with this was the way in which, in certain industries, the introduction of women workers into areas of work formerly dominated by men encouraged the conceptualization of women as unskilled workers – women appeared to be the representatives of the means by which skill dilution was achieved. In reality, changes in the labour process extended the opportunities for the employment of non-apprenticed workers and in such circumstances employers seized the opportunity to employ cheap female labour. But the antagonisms and hostilities which arose between male and female workers compounded the difficulties faced by women seeking to insist on their skills and value as workers.

Underlying these divisions between male and female workers was the prevailing view, held by many men, that women's proper place was in the home or, at least, that certain work was, and should remain, 'men's work'. Moreover, because it was the practice to pay very low wages to women, understandably men saw in women workers a threat to their own wage rates. These divisions and hostilities which often characterized the working relationships between men and women similarly tended to reinforce the rigid nature of the sexual division of labour. Men were willing to use their collective power to insist on the maintenance of a distinction between the areas of women's work and men's work. [...]

The social processes which structured women's location and experiences within the local labour market and the limitations of Liverpool's industrial structure were vividly revealed by the economic crisis of the inter-war years [...] Indeed, this was a decisive historical period for women workers and for the future shape of the sexual division of labour. A number of tendencies with regard to the changing outline of the sexual division of labour and its effects on women were consolidated in this period.

The history of the weakness in women's trade union organization in the period before the 1930s ill-equipped women to counter capital's attempts to increase the exploitation of labour at this time. Indeed, women workers were undoubtedly a prime target in this project [...] The transformations which took place in a number of workplaces in the city were pushed through, it appears, with little resistance. The concentration of women workers at the lower levels of the occupational hierarchy was effectively crystallized.

The other major tendency with regard to the sexual division of labour brought to fruition in the circumstances of the inter-war depression was the consolidation of a relationship between women workers and the personal service industry. Waged domestic work was widely upheld as the solution to female unemployment [...] unemployment legislation became one agency through which this was achieved. Trends in the previous decades indicated a shift of women workers away from domestic work. Moreover, the widespread dissatisfaction amongst women over the conditions of employment in resident domestic service had become a major public issue. But in the circumstances created by mass unemployment, domestic work was again regarded as the most appropriate career for women workers. Social policy both reflected and reinforced this view concerning the proper location for women within the occupational structure. Both directly and indirectly state intervention upheld a conventional ordering of the sexual division of labour. For the women workers of Liverpool the imperatives of this policy, combined with a limited labour market, even further diminished, tended to intensify these national tendencies. For many thousands of local women who lost their jobs at this time there was simply no alternative to employment in domestic work or a retreat into the home.

The experience of mass unemployment was to raise another factor which distinguished men's and women's relationship to the labour market. Male unemployment was at the centre of the political debates of the period and the tragic consequences of unemployment for men were given prominence at the time. Female unemployment did not, however, arouse the emotions, anger, moral condemnation and political urgency attached to male unemployment. The refusal to accept women's unemployment as genuine and important underpinned government responses to it. This was reflected in unemployment legislation. The corollary of the prevailing ideology which placed women firmly in the home was the expression of a refusal to accept women's rights to work and a denial of the genuineness of women's unemployment. Just as women's experiences and rights at work were constrained within gender ideologies, so unemployed women were regarded as a special case, distinct from unemployed men. The financial needs of women, and the importance of their income to others dependent on them, were issues consistently ignored in this period. The needs of the male breadwinner were asserted at women's expense. Women became the hidden unemployed of the inter-war years. Forced back into the home and into jobs which lacked a public presence, their interests and aspirations were conveniently buried. [...]

This study has sought to indicate that for the women workers of Liverpool the experience of the period between 1890 and 1939 was one of continuity, only briefly interrupted in the decade between 1910 and 1920, when the female labour market briefly opened out beyond its traditional boundaries. For many women in the city the entire period was continuously defined by the experience of limited opportunity for dignified, well-remunerated work. The tendency for a rigid sexual division of labour to be continuously reproduced was sustained by a series of complex and interlocking social processes evident within diverse areas of social life, from the policies and practices of trade unions, employers and governments to people's very sense of themselves as men and women, masculine and feminine. [...]

Source: unpublished Ph.D. thesis, University of Liverpool

Reading B: Kevin McManus, 'Céilís, Jigs and Ballads: Irish Music in Liverpool'

The roots of irishness

I think Irish music is a part of me that couldn't be expressed in any other way. I think there's an emotional and spiritual fulfilment that comes from it. I suppose it's something to do with being Irish …

> (Lennon et al., 1988, p.74)

Liverpool, long renowned for its Irishness, was at one time referred to, on both sides of the Irish Sea, as 'the capital of Ireland'.

[...]

Today the [city's] Irish Centre is as important as ever to the local Irish community. There is probably no better opportunity to witness this than on a Sunday lunchtime when the building is a hive of activity and filled with people of all ages. Irish papers are sold in the shop and provide topics of conversation, an Irish band plays in the main hall, while Comhaltas have their classes for teaching young people Irish music. There is also an Irish language class for children.

Tommy Walsh [one of the founders of the Irish Centre] gives one small example of the many ways in which the Centre promotes a sense of Irishness.

People who never had the remotest interest in the Irish language, even though their background was Irish, came in and when they saw the signs over the toilets saying 'Fir' for men and 'Mna' for women, and 'Oifig' over the office door, and so on and so forth, it reminded them when they were kids that they learnt these things. There was a getting away from the idea that people have in any other country, whether it be England or America or wherever, that if you want to make something look Irish then you paint it green … You didn't see shamrocks, but you saw things like the
Claddagh symbol, the St Brigid's Cross, the Round Tower, things like that. It was more subtle, if you like, and it was carefully thought out. Irish people taking their English friends in had to explain to people the significance of things. Now that in itself made them feel good.

Shay Black, who leads the popular music session at the Centre every monday night, makes another point:

It's definitely important that the Irish have some sort of building that is perceived as Irish, without ghettoizing people. But you don't need to ghettoize the Irish because the Irish are in all parts of Liverpool society …

[...]

Irish traditional music

Traditional music can be defined many ways, but its fundamental characteristic is one of direct transmission. That is, the music is learned from the performances of others, and players of one generation learn from the next in this manner. In the face of global popular music trends, Ireland retains a vigorous, orally transmitted musical tradition.

The national repertoire in Ireland today is rooted in the popular music of Ireland of the Seventeenth and Eighteenth centuries. It consists of instrumental music, mostly dance music, but also songs in Irish and English.

[...]

The rise of the dance hall led to the creation of the céilí band. To adapt their music for the dance halls, musicians had to become louder and have a heavier and more rhythmic backing, so the classic line up of a céilí band evolved to a fiddle, flute, accordion, piano and drums. (The word céilí refers to the practice of gathering in a neighbour's house for chat, story telling, and sometimes dancing.)

The prototype for what became the céilí band first emerged amongst the Irish emigrant groups in England and America at the start of the twentieth century, and it was then adopted in the home country.

This parallels the theory of historian Roy Foster, who believes that 'Ireland claimed a fiercely and unrealistically obsessive identification from its emigrants' (quoted in O'Connor, 1991, p. 62). This 'obsessive identification' ensured that a musical tradition, long in the doldrums in Ireland, would live to go back home.

Another side to this argument is that colonialism stripped the native Irish of their culture, and music is significant because it was an important way of preserving cultural memory and transmitting it across generations.

The Irish emigrant faces contradictory pressures – on one hand, to become assimilated into the new country, and on the other to affirm exclusive Irishness. Music can play an important role dealing with such pressures as the following quotation from Brid Boland, a woman who left Ireland in the 1980s, shows:

I know that a lot of people didn't have an interest in Irish music before they left Ireland and they started developing it then. Somehow or other it seems that music goes beyond words, that it is easier to tap into as a way of identifying what your difference is, and it expresses something that is very personal to you. Probably it could be done in other ways, through poetry or art or something, but it seems like music is easier. I thing it's part of the whole thing of becoming aware of what being Irish is, which you don't realize until you're placed in a situation which forces you to find out.

(Lennon et al., 1988, p. 72)

The Liverpool Céilí Band and Comhaltas

Comhaltas, or in full, Comhaltas Ceóltoirí Eireann (Association of Irish Musicians), was founded in Ireland in 1951 when traditional music there was in a state of decline and in danger of dying out. To counteract this trend a small group of idealists banded together to form Comhaltas with the aim of promoting Irish traditional music, singing and dancing. Today there are branches in every county in Ireland, thirty-six in Britain, around thirty in the United States, half a dozen in Australia, as well as branches in Sardinia, Tokyo, and Luxembourg.

The Liverpool branch, formed in 1957, is one of the oldest. Two other branches, Glasgow and West London, both strongholds of Irish emigrants, formed at around the same time.

[...]

Today there are a number of traditional Irish groups active in the Liverpool area, such as Finn's Hotel and The Carlin Céilí Band, but The Liverpool Céilí Band are probably still the most well known.

The Liverpool Céilí Band grew out of the early days of Comhaltas and was formed to enter competitions and festivals in Ireland. Its members have included Sean McNamara, Eamon Coyne, and Kit Hodge.

The name of the Liverpool Céilí Band is still renowned wherever traditional Irish music is played because the band twice (1963 and 1964) won the All Ireland competition. Sean McNamara offers one explanation of why the band were so successful:

Well, we were playing so often was one side of it. Enthusiasm. And as much as anything else we were a real well-practised céilí band because we were playing so often.

We used to play regularly at St Mary's in Highfield Street on Sunday nights and at St Cuthbert's off Prescot Road. At the time we competed, because we were playing so often at céilís, we had a great swing and rhythm which I suppose helped us to win. We always played as if for a hall full of dancers, because that was what we were used to. Liverpool has a great reputation in traditional music through the Céilí Band but also through the achievements of the youngsters. They do expect, when it comes to traditional music, a high standard from anyone that comes out of Liverpool.

[...]

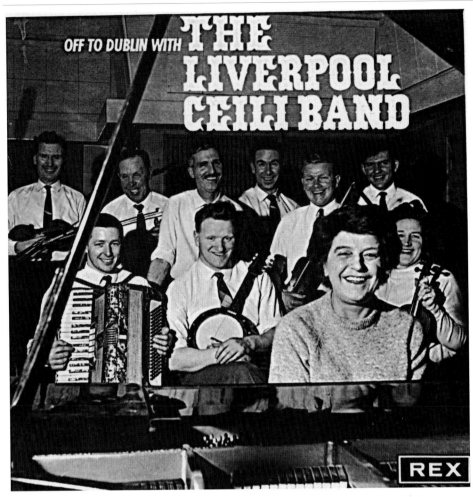

OFF TO DUBLIN WITH **THE LIVERPOOL CEILI BAND**

REX

An early Liverpool Céilí Band record celebrating their musical heritage and musical pilgrimages to Ireland

The Liverpool Céilí Band still plays today, although Stan McNamara is the only original member involved. Eamon Coyne, the other main stalwart of the band, died in 1990 but his sons, Terry and Eamon, now play in the band, thus continuing the family tradition. Kevin Webster, whose father was a member over a decade ago, also plays in the band, and Peggy Peakin, sister of another original member Kit Hodge, has been in the band since 1965.

The band are still very much in demand, with a regular monthly booking at the Irish Centre which attracts large audiences of all ages, and almost everybody joins in with the dancing. Today there are other Irish bands in Liverpool playing traditional music and a mixture of traditional/country and western.

Since the death of Eamon Coyne, the Céilí Band have not been on what used to be regular trips to Ireland, but whenever any of these musicians get together tales of those trips come flooding out. Liverpool's Irish musicians always seem to place great store in playing in the 'home' country, and the trips are remembered as being great fun, as Terry Coyne recalls …

The band always consisted of about 15 members by the time we got over there, about eight from here and we picked up seven while we were over there. Most nights we ended up with about thirty people on stage sitting around, playing music. The actual situation, when you do go over, is you all meet up with the people that you've known and you'll go out and you'll find a pub and you'll play all day and you'll love it.

Visiting Ireland is one very visible way in which Irish Identity is expressed, and the trips to Ireland organized by P.J.McCarthy, the Irish-born singer with Cream of the Barley (the leading Irish pub band in the city) emphasizes the strength of the links between Liverpool and Ireland and the importance people place on this link.

We used to have a great time years ago when the boat went from Liverpool. We'd do these trips to Dublin and there would be 200 or so of us going and it would be unbelievable. We had some great days there and there's some unbelievable stories. We brought extra people back with us, we lost people, all sorts of things.

We used to play on the boat. The first time we ever went there were 200 of us in the bar which was only meant to hold 150. We were going to play all night and we had different people with us who were going to get up. We decided we'd start playing when the boat left and begin with 'The Leaving of Liverpool' just to be really on the ball.

The boat was due to leave at ten o'clock and at about quarter past it starts vibrating and we thought it was going so we started singing. We finished off at about 11.15 and looked out and we hadn't even moved. We were knackered and we hadn't even started!

[...]

Tunes and pints: Liverpool sessions

In Liverpool, a good deal of traditional Irish music-making takes place in a fairly informal setting, which generally goes under the name of a 'session.'

For people expecting the usual 'stage/band/audience' format, the session is a surprise. Players play together, for each other, with an intrinsic part of the tradition being that there is no audience in the usual sense, rather an extended group with musicians and listeners alike included in the music-making.

Liverpool musician Eamon Coyne gives an impression of how a session works: 'It doesn't matter where you go (in Ireland),

you can walk into a pub where there's some musicians playing, and you can walk straight in, not knowing them, and within five minutes they'll be buying you a pint and you'll be playing tunes with them. That's the good thing about it. That's the thing with trad; it's very social.'

The most well attended traditional Irish music session in Liverpool today takes place every Monday night at the Irish Centre. The large numbers attending this session give an indication of the strength of traditional Irish music in the city.

[...]

Old songs in new pubs

[...] Irish music in the pubs is a relatively recent phenomenon, beginning in 1984 when a local businessman, Bob Burns, opened a pub in Matthew Street called Flanagan's Apple. Now, in 1994, you can hear a band playing Irish music in an Irish-style Liverpool city centre pub any night of the week. The names of the pubs (Flanagan's, Guinan's, Kitty O'Shea's, Rosie O'Grady's) and the bands (Cream of the Barley, Black Velvet, The Hooleys, Blarney Stone) leave little doubt as to what to expect from these establishments.

It is interesting that these same (or similar) pub names can be found across the world, in cities such as New York, Boston, Sydney, even Prague, where Irish expatriates and Irish music fans gather.

In many ways these popular pubs have transformed nights out in Liverpool city centre for many people. Everyone now knows where Flanagan's is and what goes on there, but this wasn't always the case, as McCarthy from Cream of the Barley explains:

In the beginning you couldn't explain to anyone where Flanagan's was. Now you can tell them where the town hall is from Flanagan's.

[...]

Today there is music seven nights a week at Flanagan's, and the pub has even expanded, opening a third floor four or five years ago. The Flanagan's formula proved so popular that owner Bob Burns has opened four more pubs (Guinan's, Rosie O'Grady's, Kitty O'Shea's and the Slaughterhouse) in the last few years.

There are a number of reasons why the Irish pub scene has taken off so quickly and in such a big way in Liverpool. Nuala O'Connor, in *Bringing It All Back Home*, cites the success in the 1980s of bands like The Pogues, The Waterboys, and Van Morrison who all brought Irish music to young mass audiences. (although in the case of Cream of the Barley, they are in fact closer to groups like The Dubliners and The Clancys than to The Pogues.)

The Pogues and Shane MacGowan took traditional and folk-based Irish music and fired it in the crucible of modern Irish emigration ... they played a chaotic set of stock Irish rebel tunes in London clubs. Pogues music represented children of the Sixties born after Carlow building workers had set up home with Mayo nurses. They rejected the anodyne ballad culture their parents identified with. The Pogues showed a way in which they could be Irish in Britain. The music was exciting and contemporary in form and culture, yet it was culturally familiar also.

(O'Connor, 1991, p. 158)

This may have applied in Liverpool, where many people in their twenties and thirties may well have been aware of their Irish background but perhaps could not see how music like the traditional music at the Irish Centre could have any relevance to them. By the time Flanagan's came along, many young people were quite happy to stand there proclaiming their Irish roots and singing along to 'Whisky In The Jar'.

Today, St Patrick's night is probably celebrated with just as much vigour in Liverpool as it is in Dublin. Flanagan's and the other Irish pubs are packed from early evening. For one night it suddenly seems as though everybody in Liverpool is Irish and proud of it.

Flanagan's: one of Liverpool's Irish pubs

Elvis Costello (who was himself born into the Irish community of Birkenhead) has described The Pogues' music as 'a promise of a good time', and this certainly holds true for Irish pub music in Liverpool. On any night of the week Flanagan's is usually full, with an audience made up of people of all ages, but with the majority in their twenties and thirties. There is usually a lively, informal atmosphere with people shouting out requests, joining in with the songs, and sometimes dancing.

Most bands playing in Flanagan's will typically include in their repertoire songs such as 'Leaving of Liverpool', 'Wild Rover', 'Whisky In The Jar', 'Black Velvet Band', and 'Seven Drunken Nights'.

Cream of the Barley's P.J. McCarthy makes an interesting point about the band's material.

A lot of the material we play is almost indigenous because with a lot of the songs people just know them and they don't even know why they know them. They don't even know where they heard them – they've just been around that long. They've been brought up in that environment where someone else was singing when they were a kid and you get people going 'Oh I know that song,' although they've never learnt it. They've never bought a record with it on, they just know it.

[...]

Liverpool – the capital of Ireland?

In a survey carried out in Liverpool in 1988, Elizabeth Ives asked the respondents (a mixture of first-, second- and third-generation Irish) how they ranked in importance various dimensions of culture to Irish national identity (Ives, 1988). She found that Irish music and dance were seen as the most important, followed by Catholic religion, although she admits that, to some extent the ordering of the attributes reflects 'exportability' and the priorities of popular culture.

Irish music (via Comhaltas, the radio, and on records or cassettes), dance (via the Irish Centre) and religious institutions are more accessible to the Irish in Liverpool, as well as being of importance to national self image in Ireland, than are Irish books or the occasion to use the Irish language.

(Ives, 1988, p.299)

Liverpool may no longer be able to lay claim to the title 'the capital of Ireland', but the recent boom in Irish pub music demonstrates the strength of the latent 'Irishness' that exists in the city. It is an Irishness so deeply engrained in the history of the city that it is never likely to disappear.

References

IVES, E. (1988) *The Irish in Liverpool: A Study of Ethnic Identification and Social Participation*, unpublished MA thesis, University of Liverpool.

LENNON, M. et al. (1988) *Across the Water: Irish Women's Lives in Britain*, London, Virago Press.

O'CONNOR, N. (1991) *Bringing It All Back Home*, London, BBC Books.

Source: McManus, 1994a, pp. 1, 10–11,13, 14–15, 19–21, 23, 31, 33–4, 37

Reading C: *Kevin McManus, '"Nashville of the North": country music in Liverpool'* __

Country music first began to emerge as a distinct commercial genre in the Southern states of 1920s America with the rise of musicians like Jimmie Rodgers, often regarded as 'The Father of Modern Country'. It flourished during the 1930s on radio barn dances and grew even more popular during the 1940s and 1950s with the emergence of stars such as Ernest Tubb, Hank Williams, Elvis Presley and Johnny Cash. Since then, country has spawned a host of household names including Patsy Cline, Tammy Wynette, Willie Nelson and Dolly Parton.

If we go further back we find that hillbilly music evolved out of a reservoir of folksongs, ballads and instrumental pieces brought to North America by the Anglo Celtic immigrants. It gradually absorbed influences from other musical sources, including the culture of African Americans, and in the socially conservative South, especially around the Appalachian Mountain region, a music emerged from the area's folk culture. This was the beginning of country music.

It is generally accepted that the first British country music emerged from Liverpool. How did this music from the 'hillbilly' Southern states of America become so popular in a British city?

Joe Butler, who has played in country bands in Liverpool since 1958 and hosted a popular country music radio show for twenty years, offers the most widely accepted view.

Liverpool is known to this day as the biggest place for country in Britain. At the time we started, there was no country anywhere else at all. A lot of it had to do with the fact that Liverpool is a seaport and people could get friends or relatives on ships to bring records from the States that you couldn't get in the UK. You still get records brought back from the States that way.

This is a view reinforced by Hank Walters, a retired docker who is generally regarded as The Father of Liverpool Country.

In Liverpool at the time (1950s and '60s) there was a massive merchant navy community that went to the States. We used to call them Cunard Yanks. A Cunard Yank was a guy who went to the States for ten days and came back with an American accent, loud ties and a baseball cap. But they also brought records back with them.

Kevin McGarry, lead singer with the Hillsiders, explains what happened to the records brought home by the local seaman.

Hardly any people today will still have the old country records because one album would do five or six streets. Someone would get it and say 'have you heard this Hank Snow album?' and it would get passed around.'

So the fact that Liverpool was the direct route for shipping traffic from America clearly had a great deal to do with why country music emerged there first. Additionally, the fact that the city was a port ensured that Liverpool was a cosmopolitan, open-minded place receptive to new ideas and new musics. The sea also offered local people the prospect of employment and the chance to broaden their horizons. As Kenny Johnson (another long-established musician and country DJ) puts it: 'It was the same reason as why Merseybeat started here; because of the seamen. We used to get the soul records and the rock and roll records long before anyone else got them just because we were here and the sailors would bring them.'

Carl Goldby (usually called 'Goldie' in country music circles), another important figure in this history, bought his first guitar while on a voyage to New Zealand and learned to play it on board ship. Bunter Perkins, stalwart of The Blue Mountain Boys, was a ship's cook. He also bought his first guitar in New Zealand after a voyage on *The Tamorowa*.

Hank Walters, who spent most of his working life on the docks, traces the Cajun influence in his music back to his grandfather who jumped ship (the *Alice Aleigh*, the biggest sailing ship ever to sail out of Liverpool) and lived for a while in Louisiana.

Tony Allen, the original lead singer with The Blue Mountain Boys, remembers getting his first country records off his old brother, who was a merchant seaman. Later, when he went to sea himself, he was taught to play guitar while on board ship.

Bernie Green, Allen's replacement in the Blue Mountain Boys, left country music for almost a decade at one point in his career to work on the North Sea before he was drawn back into country.

The bug came back through listening to music on board. They were all lads from the Southern states, so they were very country oriented. We had a few jam sessions and then I got the urge again and came back to it.

Joe Butler points out a second possible factor in why country music took off in

The Blue Mountain Boys: one of Liverpool's most popular country-and-western bands in the 1960s (photographed in 1963)

Liverpool, citing further American influences from the neighbouring Burtonwood American Air Base.

They used to have country on regularly there. They used to bring bands in from the States and various musicians went into the base. That and sailors bringing records home from the States were the biggest factors as to why it started in Liverpool.

Hank Walters, Kenny Johnson and Bernie Green all played at Burtonwood. Johnson remembers the jukebox there featured the likes of Ernest Tubb, Webb Pierce and Hank Williams.

Green recalls being asked to play at the base sometime around the mid-1950s.

We (The Drifting Cowboys) were approached by the staff sergeant from Burtonwood. He took us to the base and we ended up playing there about twice a week for the following four years in the Servicemen's Club – one night in the GI club and one night in the officer's mess.

We must have been doing something right because we were there for three or four years. At the time (the US airmen) couldn't believe it because we sang in an American style. We got on like a house afire. They in their turn gave us a load of records, so the learning material was endless. It helped us enormously. We might be getting say £10 local but when we went to play for them we were getting three times that amount and all you could eat.

So Liverpool's early pre-eminence in British country music could be explained to a large extent by the city's unique position as a port trading with the United States, and to a lesser extent by the proximity of Burtonwood Air Base. On the other hand it could be something much simpler:

Country music could be sung by a whole load of people, and that's what they like here.

(Hank Walters)

Source: McManus, 1994b, pp. 1–4

Global worlds

by John Allen

Chapter 3

3.1 Thinking in a global frame

As the title suggests, this chapter is about all things global. In the previous chapter, we considered local worlds, in particular the local world of Liverpool, within the context of global connections. One of the main arguments presented there was that it is impossible to understand the changing fortunes of Liverpool, or for that matter any place, outside of the wider connections which constitute it. The global in this sense *is* the variety of interconnections which over time give shape to different parts of the world. Other senses of the global are possible: for example, that of an environmentally fragile world coming apart at the seams in the face of economic progress, or that of a political world order loosely held together by the most powerful nations. These too, however, take their shape from the variety of social relationships which stretch across the globe, linking together the fortunes and prospects of different peoples. Here, we want to explore this notion of the global a little further by taking a closer look at the kind of ties and connections between places which, for many today, are regarded as an unmistakable sign of the global times in which we live. It is as if what happens to us in our everyday lives – in the kinds of work that we do, what we eat and how we relax – is somehow bound up with all kinds of things going on elsewhere across the globe. It is as if the world today has, in a commonplace sense, become *more* global.

Let me put this another way. We are constantly being told that the work which goes into the products we buy in our local shopping centre takes place in a variety of locations worldwide. Nothing is made in one place any more. A new product is financed in Japan, designed in Europe, assembled in Indonesia and marketed by an advertising agency in the UK. We hear stories about information-rich 'superhighways' which have the ability to link the world's people together in some kind of 'global village'. We expect to be able to buy strawberries and other perishables all year round, from any number of far-off locations, at our local supermarkets. I could go on with this line of thought, but the direction is clear. What, then, does it mean to say that the world today has become increasingly global? How would you start to answer this question?

Well, one way is to suggest that the global web simply has far more connections or strands to it than before. If, say, millions of people in Indonesia, Malaysia, Mexico or Ghana, or wherever, feel that their culture or their livelihoods are now directly affected by what happens elsewhere in a way that was not the case before, then the world could, in that sense, be said to be more of a global place today. More people are connected, so to speak. Another possibility is to speak about a world that is increasingly global simply because we know about what is happening elsewhere sooner or more swiftly than before. In a world of electronic highways and satellite communications, and the computerization of this and that, our knowledge of other parts of the world could be said not only to have increased, but also to have speeded-up. In this sense, it is possible to think of ourselves as close to everywhere.

These possibilities are the kinds of issues that we will be exploring later in the chapter. One thing that we can be confident about at the outset, however, is that the global is not an altogether novel phenomenon.

Consider, for example, that strange mix of travellers, merchants and pilgrims who crossed the vast cultural spaces of the globe, at a time before the railways and other modern forms of transport and communication were in place. The global for them, as it is for us, as Chapter 1 pointed out, is what we have come to know. It is precisely those connections which are known, that are taken up and invested with meaning. The same is true of the ties of economic trade, political conquest and cultural domination which gave shape to the complex colonial worlds of the seventeenth and eighteenth centuries referred to in Chapter 2. From the standpoint of a colonial administrator in the Indian Civil Service or a sugar plantation owner in the Caribbean, the world at that time took its shape and meaning from the economic, political and cultural relationships which bound them into the globe. The global in that sense only becomes known *in and through* such relationships. And, as Chapter 2 also pointed out, the changing geography of such relationships is what has given shape to successive phases of globalization.

Globalization has taken a succession of historical forms, dating back, according to some commentators, to the earliest forms of exploration, trade and plunder in the sixteenth and seventeenth centuries. As the nature of these ties and connections has changed, so too has the form of globalization. Globalization here refers to the fact that people in various parts of the world, which hitherto may have been largely unaffected by what happened elsewhere, now find themselves drawn into the same *social space* and effectively governed by the same *historical time*.

globalization

social space
historical time

One way of expressing this is to say that the connections drawn between people and events across the globe tie them in to the same sweep of historical time. In the case of the various colonial worlds, for instance, this effectively meant tying parts of the non-European world into the rhythms, movements and subjugations of the Spanish, Portuguese, Dutch, French and British Empires. Over the years, the diverse history of much of the non-European world was progressively brought within the time-frame of the West. So for the Mayan Indians in what is now Belize in Latin America the contact with other cultures, first the Spanish and then the British, locked them into a set of meanings and practices which owed little to their own time and much to the time of Europe. Vast tracts of the globe became part of distinctive imperial geographies; that is, part of a social space which shaped the everyday lives of people and their long-term fortunes (see Figure 3.1 and Plate 6). Being part of the social space of the West effectively hooked them into the same historical time.

How far then, to return to the main question, do these notions of social space and historical time help us to understand a world that is said to be becoming *more* global?

A number of points raised can help us to get to grips with this question.

In the *first* place, echoing thoughts expressed in Chapter 1, the very notion of the global is dependent upon which set of connections is taken up and invested with meaning. So the idea that the world is increasingly global or, to put it another way, that more and more of the globe has been drawn into a single world depends, in part, upon which connections are highlighted. The world view of the unemployed docker in Liverpool is likely to differ from that of the well-to-do travel writer, as will both from those forced to eek out a subsistence living in an ex-French colony in central Africa.

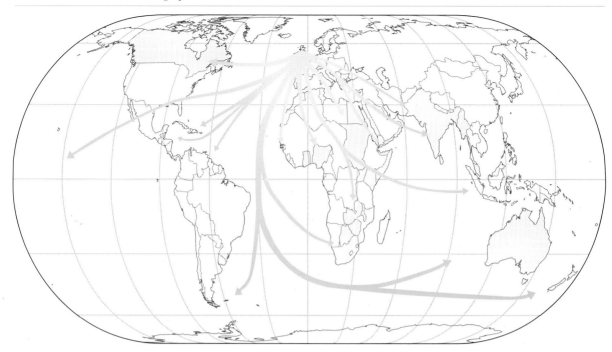

Figure 3.1   *Tied into imperialism: the social space of the British Empire*

Second, many of the global connections which are drawn to our attention would appear to lock together parts of the world in ways that alter our sense of distance. So today, if what happens in one part of the world is jarred by distant events elsewhere, such as an ecological catastrophe or the crash of an international bank, or should instantaneous communications enable some people to be closer to one another half way across the globe than to their downtown neighbours, then our experience of time and space has been compressed. The world, so to speak, has shrunk in size as distant places appear closer, accessible even – despite the long distances involved. Our experience of what happens in other parts of the globe is thus said to be more intense, more immediate in character.

Third, globalization today, if it is not simply a re-run of past experiences, should involve something qualitatively different about how places and people are drawn into the social space of others and actively hooked into the same historical time. The experience of inequality may be far from new, but the nature of the connections should shape the experience of inequality in new and rather different ways. If you are living or working in New York or in Beijing, you should be aware that the ways in which you relate to other people and places across the globe have altered in a profound sense.

The period we are concerned with here is the latter half of the twentieth century as it spills over into the twenty-first. In the remainder of this chapter we will be considering, first, a number of *representations* of globalization which have attracted much attention of late, principally because they seem to offer some understanding of what is happening around us worldwide. Thereafter, in section 3.3, we will take a closer and somewhat critical look at the *global geographies* that underpin the different conceptions of globalization and their forms of interconnection. Attention will be drawn to who is and who is not making the connections and thus, by extension, whose global imagination is at work.

Section 3.4 draws together some concluding observations on the nature of our geographical imaginations in what for some is a truly global world and for others merely the West's and increasingly the East's – that of East Asia in particular – *social space.*

3.2 Globalization: out-of-scale images

By *out-of-scale images* (following Said, 1994), I mean that there are certain images of globalization which are more suggestive than others and which have made it difficult to entertain other, perhaps less compelling, images. These out-of-scale images have a certain pull on our imagination, and direct attention to some interconnections and ties, whilst leaving others less in focus. Such images are not categorically wrong, however; they are simply partial. To refer to them as one-sided, though, fails to convey their out-of-scale character. Rather, they are *distorted* ways of making sense of a changing world and its geography; in much the same way that a mirror is capable of distorting images. Some characteristics are overblown, for example, whereas other features appear as less significant than they actually are. Thus if we fail to see the latter, it is probably because it is the former that captures our attention. Equally important to note, too, is the fact that the images are drawn from a particular vantage point.

out-of-scale images

The first image that we will explore is that of a form of *economic* globalization, namely that of a world in which borders are crossed and distances traversed with minimal effort by firms, currencies and commodities. Here, the most dynamic firms are said to organize themselves at a global scale, servicing global markets from any number of locations in the world. Another image of globalization, one which stresses *cultural* forms and patterns, draws attention to the convergence of cultural styles as Western forms of consumption spread across the globe. If it is not all kinds of people tugging at the ring-pulls of cola cans across the globe, then a similarly vast range of nationalities is to be seen taking a bite from a Big Mac. This is, of course, to slip into the realm of caricature, although the basis of a global culture starts (even if it does not end) with such icons. Finally, a third representation of globalization is *political* in its thrust and points to the continuing erosion of the nation state's powers and abilities to control or regulate an increasingly volatile and uncertain global world. In this scenario, it is the effectiveness of the nation state which has diminished in the face of environmental or security risks, for instance, and the rise of transnational agencies or organizations on the world stage which has accompanied the decreasing significance of nation states.

These accounts represent three 'takes', as it were, on the shape of globalization in the current era. Whilst it is apparent that each approaches the question of globalization from a quite different direction – the economic, the cultural and the political – it will become equally clear that they draw on the substance of each of the other 'takes'. Having said that, we shall see later just how divergent are their global geographies.

3.2.1   An economic world without borders

borderless world

The notion of a *borderless world* delivers perhaps a misleading impression of what some proponents of economic globalization wish to convey; namely, the free movement of goods, money, labour, technology, or just about anything you care to mention, across the borders of the nation state. In fact, a global economy is not so much borderless as one in which the regulatory barriers erected by nation states to prevent the free flow of goods and services have fallen sufficiently to enable firms to trade, invest and earn profits wherever they choose. In doing so, however, the borders that matter are those created by the major economic players on what, to all intents and purposes, is regarded increasingly as a 'level playing field'. In a world of falling political and spatial barriers, as the so-called electronic highways enable firms to organize their activities across vast distances, capital will move to and create its own economic zones. This is what Kenichi Ohmae, the author of a best-selling book entitled *The Borderless World* (1990), has to say about such economic zones:

They may or may not fall within the geographic limits of a particular nation – whether they do is an accident of history. Sometimes these distinct economic units are formed by parts of states, such as those in northern Italy, Wales, Catalonia, Alsace-Lorraine or Baden-Württemberg. At other times they may be formed by economic patterns that overlap existing national boundaries, such as those between San Diego and Tijuana, Hong Kong and southern China, or the 'growth triangle' of Singapore and its neighbouring Indonesian islands. In today's borderless world these are natural economic zones and what matters is that each possesses, in one or another combination, the key ingredients for successful participation in the global economy.

(Ohmae, 1993, p. 79)

A key ingredient in this case is the willingness to embrace the liberalization of trade, investment and capital movements. Thus successful integration into the global economy is achieved through the elimination of barriers to the cross-border activities of firms. On this kind of economic map, therefore, the boundaries of the nation state are as clear as ever, yet of little practical significance, especially to global firms.

Global firms are regarded as the driving force behind economic globalization (Dicken, 1992). Now there is much that is misunderstood about global firms. For a start, it does not mean that for a firm to be bestowed the label 'global', it should be seen to trade and invest in a multitude of locations worldwide. The same coloured dots appearing on a map of the world, in each and every continent, do not make a company global. The dots, for instance, may represent nothing more than distribution or sales outlets for a product made in the firm's parent country. Rather, before a firm may be considered global, many of these dots would have to represent the whole range of a company's activities in *each* location. That means having a full production presence, research and development (R & D) facilities, a management presence, as well as marketing and distribution facilities in each of the firm's major markets across the globe.

Figure 3.2 gives an idea of what the United Nations (UN) Programme on Transnational Corporations (or TNCs) thinks such a firm looks like. When the links between the parent company and its affiliates run from top to bottom like this, they call it *deep integration*.

deep integration

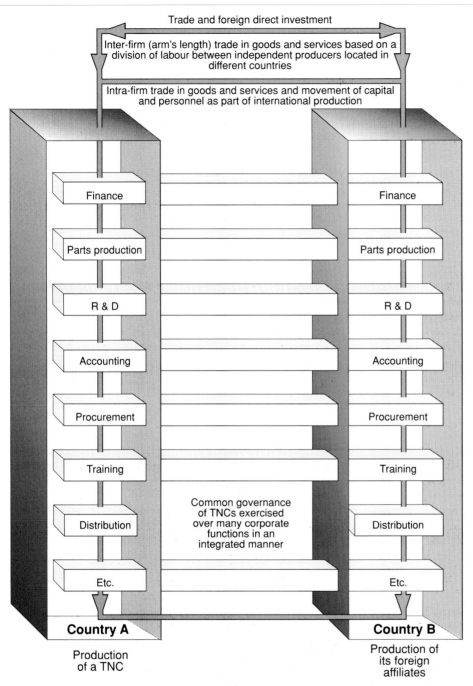

Figure 3.2 Deep integration between parent company and affiliate (Source: United Nations, 1993, p. 163, Figure VII.1.c)

Let me say, first off, that numerous examples of such firms do not spring readily to mind. There is, however, one close candidate: Asea Brown Boveri (ABB), a Swiss–Swedish electrical engineering giant. Its management structure is decentralized, with directors and executives drawn from a range of nationalities, not just from Sweden and Switzerland. It draws most of its sales from outside those two countries, much of its production takes place elsewhere, and some of its research and development functions are located in its major markets. Without probing too deeply into the precise nature of what happens where, ABB could well be a truly global company. But it is probably the exception.

Ford, the US vehicle maker, has (at the time of writing) just embarked on a radical organizational shake-up with the ultimate aim of transforming itself into some kind of borderless firm, but there is room to doubt its global claims. The Ford 2000 project, its global plan of action, divides the company into five product divisions, each responsible for the design, development, manufacture and marketing of a particular vehicle, be it a commercial truck, or a small or large car. Four out of the five divisions, however, are to be located in Dearborn, USA, near the company's headquarters in Detroit. The other divisions, responsible for small and medium cars, will be split between the UK and Germany. Other significant vehicle markets – the Latin American and especially the fast growing Asian markets – oddly enough do not figure in the plan.

How global, then, is 'global' in relation to such a company? Is it really about 'deep integration' and little else? If this is so, then why do we hear so much about globe-spanning firms? Nike, the US maker of athletic shoes, for example, subcontracts the production of its shoes to around 40 locations, most of which are in East Asia (Chinese factories being the most favoured location). The bulk of its research and development takes place at Nike's headquarters in the USA, although some – for example the product development process – is shared with subcontractors in Taiwan. The rest of the subcontractors are faxed the final shoe designs. East Asia, incidentally, according to Donaghu and Barff (1990), accounts for a small fraction of the sales of Nike's athletic shoes. How global, then, is Nike? Or take the example of the world's largest cleaning company, ISS, a Danish-based firm, with its European head office in London and a workforce of 120,000 worldwide spread across North America, Europe and parts of Latin America. Like Nike, its production is heavily reliant upon the use of labour rather than lots of capital and machinery and buildings or streams of research and development. In that sense, neither firm is capable of achieving something like 'deep integration'. Their pretensions, if indeed they have any, to become borderless firms, to source global markets through global operations, will inevitably be frustrated.

Perhaps the real candidates for the title of borderless firm are not those companies involved in manufacturing or labour-intensive services, but those operating in banking and finance. More than most, the large international banks and securities houses can lay claim to an economic world which is borderless. The way in which the big US and Japanese finance houses – the likes of a Chase Manhattan, a Citicorp or a Daiwa or Nomura – talk about 24-hour global trading on the world's currency markets or the extent to which their cross-border financial activity takes place outside of government regulation, must bring them close to the status of 'stateless firms'. Moreover, it is the world of finance, rather than that of manufacturing or services more generally, which has experienced a considerable lowering of controls on the movement of capital. Coupled with the spread of new communications technologies which have enabled money to be switched around the globe at breakneck speeds, it is the global finance houses which appear to give full expression to Ohmae's borderless geographies (Ohmae, 1990, 1993). Their financial activities may not represent the form of 'deep integration' recognized by the UN's Programme on Transnational Corporations, but it does nevertheless amount to a form of economic integration which tightly connects different locations across the globe.

But once again, how global are these finance houses? In terms of instantaneity and the pace at which information is transmitted across the globe, there has been a qualitative shift in our experience of time and space. But how much of the world is tied in to this experience? Which people and places are driving this form of economic integration and who and where is left out?

Activity 1 The next time that you come across an advertisement in a daily newspaper like the one presented in Plate 7 – usually of a globe with an array of lines drawn around it to convey the impression of connection and movement – note the locations at which the bank or security house trades its financial services. The list may not include every one of the firm's trading locations, but it will give you an idea of the geographical scope of its operations. London, New York and Tokyo inevitably will be shown, and possibly Chicago, Paris, Zurich, Singapore and Hong Kong. Osaka in Japan may also be listed, alongside perhaps Bahrain and Los Angeles, but I suspect few others.

As for the global firms mentioned earlier, especially Ford, there are only a handful of locations which have any real significance for the big finance houses on their economic maps of the world. Indeed, most of the national borders crossed by global firms of whatever kind tend to be those associated with the advanced economies of North America, Europe and East Asia. Less or even out of focus, in a global sense, are those parts of the world – for instance much of the African continent – which are either unconnected or only loosely connected to the advanced economies. Also out of focus are the connections that people from the poorer economies make as they migrate or move across the world in search of what the West has to offer. In comparison with the idea of the free movement of capital and currencies across national borders, the free movement of labour is far removed from the out-of-scale imagery of the latest wave of economic globalization.

We shall return to these and other aspects of the uneven and unequal global geographies of the economic world in section 3.3. For now, we move on to consider the next 'take' on globalization in the contemporary era: namely that of a global culture.

3.2.2   A cultural world of sameness

The idea of a *global culture* is perhaps one of the easiest ways to convey what is meant by an out-of-scale image. Think about this for a second. People all over the world these days are said to be watching the same television programmes, more often than not routine Western 'soaps'. What does that mean? Does it mean that we all make sense of the characters and 'the plot' in the same way? It is unlikely, of course. After all, the notion that we all belong to the same cultural community or that those watching *Dallas* or *L.A. Law* in a less developed part of the world attach the same meaning to them as do the folk in Fort Worth, Texas is to stretch a point. Nonetheless, and this is the key issue, there is a sense in which the exposure of local cultures to the outside world, to the influence of the global media and other forms of communication, has started to break down cultural barriers. This is not so

global culture

much an argument for a borderless culture, then, as it is for the view that much of the world is becoming the same. In short, there is a move towards a *common* global culture.

The basis of this global culture is seen to rest upon the reach of the new technologies of communication, especially that of satellite television. The ability to reach into the everyday lives of those in far-off places is a relatively recent phenomenon, and one that is said to unsettle and loosen more traditional cultural ties and influences. The Westernized satellite entertainment beamed into Indian homes, for example, may not be understood as elsewhere, but it may throw into question established lifestyle codes around dress and moral behaviour. Other more familiar forms of cultural exposure – through films, magazines and travel – are also seen to play a part in this loosening of hitherto robust local cultures. For many, however, it is the ability to transmit images and cultural messages from one part of the world to another at the touch of a button which holds out the greatest threat to local cultures.

Part of this apparent dissolution is said to stem from the exposure to different consumer cultures – often based upon US lifestyles and products – which project into the homes of the rich and poor alike across the globe the very possibility that they too can be part of one, albeit Western, world. The message on the radio or television which speaks across linguistic and cultural communities is that they too can also gain access to the consumer trappings of the advanced economies; if they have not already started to do so in the shape of a pair of Nike trainers or a Ford motor car or pick-up.

global standardization   At one extreme, this demand is produced by the global marketing of cultural styles and symbols and is met, according to Kevin Robins (1991), by the *global standardization* of products. On this view, it is not that everyone, regardless of the amount of money at their disposal or where they come from, is seduced into wanting the same cultural products, but rather that the large global firms target groups of consumers with similar tastes in different parts of the world and service that demand globally. Not everyone wants to be clad in expensive running shoes, for instance, but there are groups of young consumers in the USA, Europe, Latin America and East Asia who do. Or so it would seem.

On another level, however, the message of a common global culture is one that has been strongly resisted by local and national cultures, especially if it bears the traits of North American culture. Take, for instance, the furore that erupted in France at the end of 1993 over the threat to allow open access to foreign films and television programmes. Interpreted by French politicians as an attempt by the United States to dilute their national culture through a less than subtle form of Americanization, the global trade talks (the GATT negotiations) became the site of resistance to the possibility of cultural imperialism, US style.

Activity 2   Read the newspaper report by Charles Bremner on this aspect of the General Agreement on Tariffs and Trade (GATT), which originally appeared in *The Times* and is reproduced opposite. Regardless of what you think about the drive to ensure linguistic purity or the appeal to the peoples of the old French Empire, it is interesting to note the strength of the perceived threat to French culture from outside. The idea of French-speakers everywhere being force-fed a cultural diet of Hollywood images is certainly an evocative one.

Mitterrand enlists old empire in linguistic defence of Gaul

FROM CHARLES BREMNER
IN PARIS

For generations, Africans and Asians in the French empire were taught to recite from history books that spoke of "our ancestors the Gauls". In an irony not lost on the colonial descendants, President Mitterrand has spent the past few days pleading with them to help France defend its language and culture against American "imperialism".

M Mitterrand managed to win endorsement, though sometimes lukewarm, from the 46 member states of the francophone community to back France's demand for "cultural exception", excluding "audiovisual goods" from the General Agreement on Tariffs and Trade. "France feels threatened and indeed it is," he told the biennial francophone summit in Mauritius, a body which represents 3 per cent of the world population. "We would be suddenly very poor and defenceless, if you were not there at our side ... who can be blind today to the threat of a world gradually invaded by an identical culture, Anglo-Saxon culture, under the cover of economic liberalism?"

In an emotional speech, he wondered: "Are the laws of money and technology about to achieve what the totalitarian regimes failed to do?" The enemy of all French-speakers was the attempt to force-feed the planet with images of Hollywood.

Boutros Boutros Ghali, the UN secretary-general, tried to calm things down with a call for diversity in language, but it did little to quell the passion now firing the French defence. Edouard Balladur, the prime minister, took up Joan of Arc's sword in Paris yesterday, calling in Isabelle Adjani, Catherine Deneuve and other stars to consult on strategy for defending the French cinema.

For many in the francophone family of the developing world, ringing

declarations in defence of French culture are the return favour for generous aid from Paris. To the anger and sorrow of Paris, the effort sometimes back-fires with a display of ingratitude. The latest example came last week when students and staff at the new French-financed schools of law and medicine in Phnom Penh, the Cambodian capital, protested against having to work in French rather than English.

Others, including Quebec and French officials, say the biggest enemy of French is to be found at home inside the frontiers of Gaul. The latest blow is a decision by Airbus Industrie, the pride of French aviation, to publish the pilots' manuals for its airliners only in English. With some exaggeration, the guardians of the language say this was a symptom of the "ghettofication" of French inside France.

"Nowadays in France, the rich and the decision-makers only speak English," complained Professor Michel Serres, a leading language crusader. "The French language has become the language of the weak and the poor."

The professor was taking a pot shot at the ascendancy of English in pop music, technical professions and business which lead, among other things, the big medical institutions and business schools to conduct symposia and issue their publications in English. Alain Peyrefitte, the Gaullist party baron, said yesterday that many French were so keen on Americanising their language that they even invent their own English, coining such popular words as le tennisman. "What's the point of being more royalist than the king?" wondered M Peyrefitte.

The Québecois, who have much stricter language laws than France, are especially upset by what they see as defeatism among the fashionable Paris

"Galloricains", as they have been dubbed. "The French political-intellectual elite does not like its language enough for France to play the motor role which *la francophonie* confers on it," said a Montreal study published last month. The quotation would have come in useful for M Balladur yesterday when he called in "representative intellectuals", after the actors, and received an earful about the dangers of an anti-American witchhunt. Bernard-Henri Levy and André Glucksman, the two biggest philosopher celebrities, said they favoured the defence of French cinema but were worried about the awakening of "the old demon of anti-Americanism".

The government is now preparing the latest rear-guard action in the drive to ensure linguistic purity. Jacques Toubon, the minister of culture and *francophonie*, has already quashed state subsidies for events not held in French and is drafting a law to force officials to communicate only in French.

Source: *The Times*, 19 October 1993, p. 11

If we stand back from this account of cultural sameness for a moment, however, it is interesting to register that, so far, we have really only spoken about a loose coalition of firms and industries, media-based or otherwise, spurred on, it would seem, by segments of consumer demand, as the driving force behind the move towards a common global culture. There seem to be few other forces involved which are capable of putting together a global culture. Indeed, in the example of so-called cultural imperialism above, it is the 'laws of money and technology' which appear to be at the vanguard of the spread of Anglo-Saxon culture. This takes us back again to the asserted power and reach of global firms. Even if such power and reach were true, however, why should we believe that something like a Western or an American way of life could be spread like a cultural sheen across the globe? Acceptance of such a view is to assume that a more assertive cultural force has the ability to gloss over local histories and traditions. It suggests that, over time, cultural unevenness and local differences may be eroded.

But that is not so, as Robins and others recognize. There are two points worth stressing about this homogenizing view of global culture.

One is that it is presented in rather a monolithic manner: that we all understand and value consumer products or old American movies in the same way. There is insufficient attention given to the possibility that people in different parts of the world – different audiences so to speak – may receive and interpret the images and styles of 'another world' in a manner quite unintended by those who produced them. Here is Ulf Hannerz commenting on this very issue:

One problem with the global homogenization scenario tends to be the quality of the evidence for it. Quite frequently it is anecdotal – 'I switched on the television set in my hotel room in Lagos (or Manila, or Tel Aviv, or Geneva), and found that Dallas was on'. In a more sophisticated version, quantitative evidence is provided that on one Third World television channel or other, some high percentage of the programming is imported.

To be more completely persuasive, arguments about the impact of the transnational cultural flow would have to say something about how people respond to it. The mere fact that Third World television stations buy a lot of imported programmes, for example, often has more to do with the fact that they are cheap, instances of cultural dumping, than that audiences are necessarily enthralled with them. We may have little idea about how many television sets are actually on when they are shown, and even less what is the quality of attention [paid] to them.

(Hannerz, 1992, p. 243)

Quite simply, we have a limited understanding of how people respond to the cultural messages transmitted. Whilst the global firms may attempt to limit how we use and value their products, they can never fully close local interpretation and adaptation. The meaning invested in Nike sportswear or the reading of an American serial 'soap' television programme is marked by cultural unevenness and local difference. It is always *translated* locally.

A second and related observation on the nature of a global culture is that, rather than eroding local differences, it actually works through them. Global firms, as Robins noted, are not in the business of turning everyone into some kind of global 'look-alike'. Rather, they are in the business of targeting certain groups for certain products; they actively explore local differences and attempt to market them on a wider scale. As Robins goes on to explain:

Cultural products are assembled from all over the world and turned into commodities for a new 'cosmopolitan' market-place: world music and tourism, ethnic arts, fashion and cuisine; Third World writing and cinema. The local and 'exotic' are torn out of place and time to be repackaged for the world bazaar.

(Robins, 1991, p. 31)

This, then, provides a rather different twist to the significance of cultural unevenness and local difference. Here aspects of local culture from wherever are taken up and *re-worked* within the global market-place, albeit one that is itself segmented by style, taste and, of course, money. Indeed, it is interesting to note that this more diverse form of global culture is also one that you have to buy into. In that sense, there is nothing free about the movement of culture across borders.

The notion of a basic sameness to global culture is therefore clearly a distortion. There is no convergence of cultural styles, only a mix of cultures and identities shaped by global firms. Having said that, however, we need to reflect once more upon how exhaustive such a view is. What is left out or glossed over by this imagery? The major force behind the re-worked local and global connections, for instance, appears to be that of capital and enterprise. What of the cultural connections drawn between places by, say, the Irish diaspora mentioned in Chapter 2, or for that matter any movement of peoples over time? After all, it is not only capital which takes responsibility for the making of cultures. The mass migrations of recent times, many of them from the less developed to the developed world, have laid down their own cultural geographies across the globe. Before we pursue this issue further, however, there is one more 'take' on globalization to consider.

The 'exotic' torn out of place?: Thai cuisine in London

3.2.3   A political world beyond the nation state

Thus far, from an economic angle, we have been concerned primarily with falling regulatory barriers and a world that is said to be increasingly borderless. Then, from a cultural point of view, we traced the impact of falling barriers to what some take to be a more even, yet culturally diverse, world. In this section, we are again concerned with barriers and boundaries: on this occasion those that mark the territory of the nation state. Our concern, however, is not so much with barriers which are said to be falling as it is with barriers that are ineffective at what they do. Too much of what is happening in the world today – from global warming and nuclear arms disposal to footloose multinationals and Gulf-style wars – seems to *elude* the powers of nation states. The politics of global change is concerned with issues that are said to reach beyond the sovereignty and control of the nation state. Indeed, they testify not so much to the eclipse of the nation state, as to the ineffectual nature of state authority in the contemporary global era.

This is quite a forceful statement, so let us take a closer look at what political imagery is involved. There are a number of possible dimensions to consider.

Let us start with some of the economic interconnections raised earlier, namely those laid down by global firms and the rapid flow of money and capital around the globe.

Activity 3 Think back to what was said about the activities of globe-spanning firms and money moving around the globe at breakneck speeds in section 3.2.1. In what ways can they be said to pose a problem of authority for nation states? How, if at all, may the movement and mobility of capital and finance undermine the effectiveness of states to control what happens within their national boundaries? Make a brief note of your response before you continue.

Apart from the much-vaunted ability of global firms to close down a branch plant in one country and to transfer production elsewhere, one way is to evade local state taxation through the remission of low reported earnings and profits from their overseas branch plants. The real earnings and profits in any one country may be higher than reported and much of it concealed within transactions between parent companies and their branch plants. Whichever arrangement is adopted, the result is the same: the inability of the local host government to obtain the taxes liable from global firms in their territory.

A more familiar and frequently cited example of the state's ineffectiveness in the face of global forces, however, is perhaps that of the volatile flow of private capital across national borders which may play havoc with the best-laid plans of governments to control inflation or to influence the movement of exchange rates. Indeed, for some, it is precisely the speed and intensity at which events around the world unravel themselves which may disrupt or undermine what states can or cannot do within their own territories.

The issue of security is a case in point. We have already learnt from Chapter 1 how the Gulf War of 1991 has been described as one played out on satellite television, on a minute-by-minute basis, courtesy of the global news media. National security, for so long regarded as simply an exercise in boundary maintenance, is now said to be tied to all manner of *transboundary issues* – from environmental pollution to the threat of exclusion from vital resources such as oil. On this view, it is increasingly difficult to regard security *as* a national affair when decisions or actions taken elsewhere may have an immediate or long-term effect upon your livelihood.

transboundary issues

Consider, for example, the issues of global warming and acid rain. If you happen to live in a country which has much of its territory close to the sea level, as the Dutch or the Maldive Islanders do, then a rise in sea level, even of a small amount, due to global warming is a threat to your environmental and, indeed, economic security. Much of the cause of global atmospheric change is likely to emanate from elsewhere, from fossil fuel-burning power station emissions, vehicle exhausts and the like, but the consequences are faced directly on your territory. In that sense, the outcome of what 'they do over there' stretches beyond national borders and spills over into the lives of others who have little or no control over what kind of emissions enter the atmosphere in far-off places. The same type of environmental connection is true of acid rain too.

Staying with the environmental theme for the moment, at a broader level it has been argued that the destruction of the rainforests in the Amazon is a global issue which has damaging ecological consequences far beyond the

Destruction of the rainforests in the Amazon

frontiers of a country like Brazil. Aside from the devastation wrought upon the livelihoods of local indigenous peoples, the destruction of the rainforests has resulted in a loss of biodiversity and contributed to rapid global atmospheric change. In this context, the notion of a 'political community' transcends national frontiers and brings into question what is within and what is beyond the domestic affairs of nation states.

In the words of Simon Dalby:

The economic security of the forest dwellers is determined by the survival of the forest, not the division of it into individual, precisely demarcated plots. Security for the rest of us likewise depends increasingly on the survival of an intact global ecosystem more than the inviolability of state borders.

(Dalby, 1992, p. 515)

global politics And in response to this kind of global world, we have witnessed the rise of a new kind of *global politics* to match: that of supra-national and transnational organizations. Figure 3.3 sets out the line of argument this far.

It should be said at the outset that the growth of supra-national institutions on the world stage is not especially new. The kind of political integration between states which is apparent in such institutions as the International Monetary Fund (IMF), the European Union or the United Nations has been a feature of much of the post-1945 period. The United Nations, for instance, through its various agencies, has been involved in a wide variety of issues, from population matters and political refugees to transnational corporations and environmental programmes. The 1992 Rio Earth Summit, which agreed conventions on climatic change and on the protection of the diversity of species, took place under the United Nations umbrella, for example, as did the 1994 World Population Conference in Cairo which stressed the role of women in fertility control.

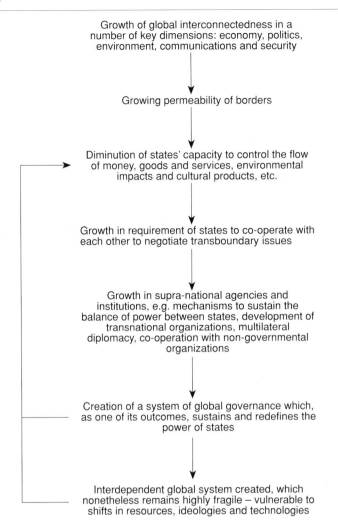

Figure 3.3 *The politics of global change in the current era (Source: adapted from Held, 1991, p. 209, Figure 8.2)*

Transnational organizations are of a different order, however. They tend to involve actors other than governments on the world stage and cut across the territorial interests of nation states. More often than not, organizations, such as Greenpeace, act in the name of the planet, drawing attention, for example, to the dumping of hazardous waste in the seas outside of territorial waters, or to the over-fishing of the oceans, or, indeed, to the despoilation of the global climate. It is the ability to speak on behalf of the 'global commons', to that web of interconnections and interdependencies which are said to affect us all, which enables such organizations to raise severe doubts over the ability of a system of states to confront global issues such as resource depletion, the food supply, nuclear waste, international debt or economic security. A politics of global change in this sense is not about 'us' and 'them', but about each and every one of us being affected in various ways by what happens elsewhere on the globe.

But at this point in the 'one world' script, we need to ask the same question of global political organizations as we did of global firms: namely, how global are they? Many of the issues that they mobilize around – for example, those of toxic waste disposal or river pollution – involve a limited number of states. Others such as global warming, as the term implies, have the potential to affect virtually all countries, although not in a uniform manner. As we have already seen, those living in low-lying countries have more to fear from global warming than, say, the various peoples in the Ethiopian highlands. If anything, in the short term the people in Ethiopia are more likely to be anxious about food shortages and entitlement rights than climatic change. So the imagery of a politics of global change is distorted in part by its attempt to speak about environmental, economic and social processes *as if* they are undeniably worldwide in scope and uniform in their impact.

Less in focus on this kind of political map are the connections which, for instance, link the disproportionate use of resources required to sustain Western lifestyles – the raw materials and energy sources – to the despoilation of the global environment and the poverty of many of those in the rest of the world who work to sustain the living standards of the developed world. While it is increasingly true that much of what is happening today 'escapes' the nation state, different parts of the world experience this phenomenon in uneven and unequal ways. But that is to run ahead of ourselves.

Summary of section 3.2

o   The three 'takes' on globalization considered here represent *out-of-scale images*; that is, they distort our understanding of global processes by drawing attention to certain ties and connections, which, in turn, make it difficult to see other kinds of relationships.

o   The central idea behind *economic* globalization is the elimination of regulatory barriers to cross-border flows of money, people, firms and commodities. Truly global firms, however, are a rare sight and so too is the free movement of labour across borders.

o   The circulation of meaning, much as the circulation of commodities, is said to have broken down cultural barriers. A common global *culture*, however, is not so much about the world becoming the same, as it is about a world of cultural difference and standardized diversity.

o   The *politics* of global change is also concerned with the growing permeability of borders, but in this instance with the inability of nation states to control what happens across them. Few global issues, however, are worldwide in scope and nation states are still key actors on the world stage.

o   Less in focus in these accounts of globalization is the *uneven* and *unequal* nature of global processes and relations.

3.3   Global geographies

We have considered three representations of globalization in the current era, each concerned with a different dimension of global change: the economic, the cultural and the political. Clearly, they overlap in various significant ways. One of these, as noted above, is the shared focus on barriers, whether they are deemed to be falling in response to worldwide pressures, overcome by global forces or simply ineffectual when confronted by global change. Another shared feature of the three accounts is the stress that they place on capital and enterprise as a dynamic of globalization. The movement and mobility of global firms across borders, the accelerated tempo of monetary flows around the world, or the ability of media-based conglomerates to get their messages across more rapidly to more people: each of these emphasizes the power of capital to shape a global world. But, as we have already indicated, this is a distorted image. Much of what is happening globally is not captured by such an image.

It is not simply that if you are a small-scale co-operative in the Caribbean producing bananas for export, you will view the barriers erected to your product in the affluent North rather differently from, say, one of the big, global fruit companies. In this case, economic globalization will indeed take on a different meaning for you. More significantly, it is also about the fact that the three representations of globalization either leave out much of what is happening in the world today and to its peoples or they tie people in in ways that reproduce unequal worlds. *Either people are not part of the same global space or, if they are tied in, the experience of inequality remains out of focus.* It is to the global geographies of these representations that we now turn.

3.3.1   Uneven worlds

That globalization has a geography could, at first glance, be construed as somewhat odd, given the all-encompassing nature of the term. As we have seen, however, there is much that is uneven about global relationships. The stress in each of the different 'takes' on globalization may well have been upon movement and flows – whether of capital, currencies, images or even pollution – but the lines of connection drawn in each case produce a markedly uneven geography.

Centred in the North ...

Let us begin with the example of economic globalization, as we drew specific attention to its skewed geography in section 3.2.1. There we spoke about the limited number of financial centres involved in cross-border financial activities. We could have added more to this picture if we had included the range of offshore financial centres, as indeed we could if we wished to map each and every bank that has ever been involved in foreign exchange dealings. Likewise, if we mapped every outlet for athletic shoes worldwide, we would have a fairly full global picture. But that would be to miss the point about economic globalization. It is not simply about everywhere being included; rather, it is about who is driving the process of globalization, where it is being driven from and the qualitative nature of the connections drawn.

If we take each of these points in turn, it is considered, as we have seen, that the global firms make the running as far as the world economy is concerned. Moreover, it is they who orchestrate the flows of investment and finance from their vantage points in the rich, industrialized economies of the North; namely those 'command' centres which have been dubbed 'global cities' – New York, Los Angeles, Tokyo, London, Paris and a small number of other centres. And such firms are able to make the running from these locations thanks to the expanding information and communications technologies which enable them to control and keep tabs on their far-flung economic interests without moving very far at all. The speed-up of communications, therefore, rather than leading to a dispersal of a firm's strategic activities, has somewhat paradoxically increased the significance of the global cities in the developed world. On this view, then, some parts of the world are pivotal to the global economy, whilst other parts, in fact many of the less developed economies, are of less significance. They are only loosely connected to the global space, so to speak.

Of course, there is far more to the global economy than this, but what is immediately apparent in this economic scenario is that the global economy is *centred* in the developed North. Consider investment and trade, for instance. These are overwhelmingly concentrated in those parts of the world that are either developed or rapidly developing, such as the fast growing economies of South and East Asia. The geographical pattern is dominated by connections drawn by the major economies of North America, Europe and Japan. American firms for the most part invest in their *home region*: that is, the USA, Canada and much of Latin America. European firms chiefly invest in their home region too: namely the countries of Western and, more recently, Eastern Europe. Likewise, Japan has stepped up its investments in East Asia, and Asian firms are generally investing in neighbouring countries. These regions are the big markets of the economic world and they represent an uneven pull on the world's commodities, investments and finance.

home region

Consider, then, what it is like to be only loosely connected to this global geography. Take the example of Ghana in West Africa. According to a recent World Bank report, Ghana's economic adjustment programme is one of the most successful on the African continent, achieving a real economic growth rate of around 5 per cent a year (World Bank, 1994). Yet at this growth rate, the World Bank observes that it will take the average Ghanaian 50 years before they cross the poverty line. In so far as Ghana is part of the global economic space of the developed world, therefore, it is connected in a subordinate way to that world. Much of sub-Saharan Africa, for example, had a higher level of wealth in real terms some 20 years ago than it has today – in the last decade of the twentieth century.

Much that has passed for the 'economics' of the developed and less developed world is perhaps best described as political economy, however. Supra-national political institutions, such as the World Bank, the IMF and GATT, alongside nation states, have played decisive roles in setting out the terms and conditions under which countries like Ghana can join the global economy. The price of connection for many of the less developed economies has involved a lowering of regulatory barriers and tariff reforms which in some cases have left them more borderless, as it were, than powerful economies such as Japan.

It will take the average Ghanaian 50 years before they cross the poverty line

... mixed up at the centre ...

In cultural terms, too, it is possible to speak about a skewed global geography: one which also could be said to be *centred* in the developed North. Cultural production, if we follow the line of thought set down earlier, is still driven by the images and messages of the first world's market-places. But it is not as straightforward as saying that North America, under the cover of economic liberalism, is making all the global cultural running. Or insisting perhaps that because Mexicans look towards US television, not European, or that the Swiss principally watch European television, not Asian satellite television, cultural influence and exposure is, like the global economy, rooted in the home region. The cultural flows and connections in the contemporary global era are more mixed and uneven in their character than this.

The starting point to this kind of thinking is the idea, expressed in section 3.2.2, that aspects of local culture and difference are re-worked for the global market-place. To be more precise, it should be market-places in the plural, as aspects of ways of life – around food, music, art, design, expression and so forth – are taken up and re-invested with meaning in a variety of ways across the world.

At its simplest, this may involve you in, say, an opportunity to sample Turkish cuisine in London. At a deeper level, however, if we stay with this example, it would require you to reflect upon – first, the migration of Turkish people to the UK in the late 1960s and early 1970s to work in the clothing industry, and second, the numbers fleeing political repression and the denial of human rights in the wake of a succession of military coups in Turkey. The two sets of connections, one the cuisine, the other the movement and migration of peoples between countries, are linked. More pointedly, they are

diaspora cultures   part and parcel of the kind of *diaspora cultures* mentioned in Chapter 2. The cultural identities that migrant groups forge represent a translation of the connections that they live in their daily lives – from a place to which many will not and some cannot return, to a negotiation of the cultures that they now live among and work alongside.

Writ large, this is another side to cultural globalization: one which tends to be just out of focus in accounts which stress the commodification of cultures. For one of the striking characteristics of the present era is precisely the wave of migrations from the less prosperous parts of the globe to the major cities of the developed and developing nations. Millions of people in the post-Second World War period have sought an economic future at the centres of the global economy: from the Caribbean basin and many Latin American countries, as well as further afield, to the USA; from Turkey and North Africa to Germany; from Indonesia and Surinam to the Netherlands; from Algeria, Tunisia and Morocco to France; from the Philippines and South Korea to Japan, and so on. Whether legal or illegal, such movements are in one sense attempts to move within the social spaces governed by the developed world.

This has at least two consequences for the notion of a global culture centred in the developed world.

The first is that the idea of a single global culture is clearly misplaced. As we have suggested, it is the *plurality* of cultures that arises from the movement and mobility of peoples as they live wider sets of global relations in the cities of the first world. We will elaborate on this point shortly. A second consequence is that the very notion of a centre is called into question as the cultures from the 'periphery' move to the core of Western social space. Here is Iain Chambers reflecting upon this question by recalling a scene from Gurinder Chadha's film *I'm British But …* (1988):

On a roof top in Southall in London, a group of Asian–British musicians are performing a song in the Bhangra style: a world beat composite of Punjab folk, Bombay film and Western disco (subsequently cross-fertilised with the black metropolises of New York and Los Angeles in Bhangra rap). They are lamenting their exile from their Punjab homeland, while down in the street other Britons of Asian descent are observing and in some cases dancing to the sound. In this doubling of a scene from twenty years previously – the Beatles playing 'Get Back' on the roof of the Apple offices – the Western stereotype is strikingly mimicked and displaced into a very different sense of history, of identity, of centre.

(Chambers, 1994, p. 87)

… and blurred at the edges

The notion of a defined centre to global relationships is also brought into question by the politics of global change. While it is true that most significant transboundary issues – from environmental risk and women's rights to international human rights or development concerns – have tended to reach the global political agenda through lobbying in the affluent world, the political process itself involves making connections or building links with groups outside of the developed world. The 'political communities' constructed around these issues, as noted earlier, transcend national frontiers; they link different groups of people in various countries on an issue-by-issue basis. Each issue in that sense lays down its own uneven geography, with some communities stretched across the globe involving a variety of organizations and agencies, and others involving no more than a handful of groups in adjacent states.

Take, for instance, the issue of international human rights. At one level, it should involve all governments in a shared global space which oversees human rights issues and curtails abuses. In practice, the political response on the world stage is made up of a number of *overlapping political communities*, from the United Nations with its Universal Declaration of Human Rights to the array of transnational organizations such as Amnesty International and a whole host of regional and local groupings, as well as various foundations. Similarly, as indicated in the previous section, the issue of environmental risk is one that connects a range of supra-national institutions and transnational agencies on the world stage, together with a plethora of small non-governmental organizations, although few of the issues are fundamentally global in scope.

overlapping political communities

On this view, then, it is hardly revealing to note the uneven character of global politics. What is of greater interest perhaps is that such politics are also *experienced* unevenly across the globe. In various parts of the world, the issue of human rights violation, for example, is not even registered, or the threat of environmental hazards is not perceived to be something to worry about unduly. Much of the response would appear to rely upon the ability of the lobbying groups or states to cajole or persuade others of the global significance of such issues. Put another way, they represent attempts to pull peoples and places, often reluctantly and with resistance, into the *same* global space. The tighter the connections and dependencies across social space, the greater is the ability to ensure political compliance. The looser the ties, the easier it is to be outside of the politics of global change.

3.3.2 Unequal worlds

No doubt it will be apparent from earlier examples, both in this chapter and before, that being tied into the social space and time-frame of the more prosperous North can be a profoundly unequal experience. If you are at the edges of the global economy, only loosely connected, as in the case of most Ghanaian households, or if you are a newly arrived migrant or refugee from an impoverished nation trying to find a place or a voice in a first world city, the experience of globalization is marked by a series of inequalities.

This is not to rehearse a familiar argument in terms of a direct clash on the world stage between blocs of economic, political or cultural power leading to a widespread pattern of global inequalities. That such clashes have been significant, especially between nation states, and that they continue to shape much of the world in the aftermath of the Cold War is undeniable. Here, however, I want to pursue a rather different line of thought; namely, what it *means* to be tied into the social space of the North on unequal terms.

The first example considers the experience of groups separated by the Atlantic Ocean, yet tied together by a product that arrives on the tables of the affluent world not long after it has been picked. The second example is somewhat different in that it focuses on peoples with different histories, cultures and memories who now face one another not, as once was, across vast distances, but across the same city or street, or even within the same workplace. In various ways, it draws upon the notion of 'local worlds' within 'local worlds' raised in the previous chapter.

Activity 4 Now turn to Reading A by Ian Cook entitled 'Constructing the exotic: the case of tropical fruit', which you will find at the end of the chapter. The reading starts out by describing what is referred to as a commodity chain; that is, the sequence of activities which, in this instance, starts as a seed at a farm in Jamaica and ends with the product displayed on a supermarket's shelves in the UK.

There are primarily three groups involved in this chain, leaving aside those who handle the cargo at different points: the farm's black workforce, the farm's white management and the supermarkets' exotic fruit buyers. Each group has something to say about their role in the chain and how they experience it. As you read through their accounts, I would like you to think briefly about how the groups on each side of the Atlantic *make sense* of the unequal connections that tie them into the same social space – economically, culturally and politically.

Well, perhaps an obvious starting point is the economic inequality inscribed in the relationship. From the buyers' point of view, the stated aim of producing a predictable stream of good fruit costing less, knowingly led to poverty wages at the other end. This acknowledgement, however, is itself interesting.

'Exotic' fruits, many of which are now commonplace, have been crossing the Atlantic for decades, but in the past distances have appeared greater and places on the far side of the ocean less accessible. Those who planted, picked and packed the fruits are largely hidden to the 'Western eye', their labour unseen behind the *barriers of distance*. Today, the Caribbean no longer seems so far away, especially to the big supermarket chains in the UK. The buyers *know* what is happening 'down the line', even if they have never actually made the journey across the Atlantic. This sense of the world becoming 'smaller' has thus forced the buyers to accommodate the reality of unequal connections. In other words, they now have an understanding of what it means to *share* the same social space and historical time.

barriers of distance

In contrast, those who work on the farms and plantations in the Caribbean have long known what it means to share the West's global space. The experience of being tied in on unequal terms holds no shocks for them, as Chapter 2 and the example of the 'triangular trade' graphically demonstrated. The difference, however, in these post-colonial times, is that the links between the Caribbean and elsewhere – whether they be through trade, investment, foreign exchange or the World Bank – are now felt more intensely and with greater speed as a result of the ability to shrink distances through high-speed transport, telecommunications and the like.

Distance, as you may have already noted, also plays a part in constructing the very meaning of the fruits. To the packers in Jamaica, the fruits were rather mundane – part of an everyday backdrop. As the fruits moved across the Atlantic, however, they became 'exotic'. Because such fruits came from far-away places it was possible to construct them as 'exotic'. But there is more to it than that.

The label 'exotic' itself has become standardized. The buyers, in response to what the supermarkets think the public in the UK will buy, specify to the fruit farmers the precise shape, size and colour of the fruits they require. In this way, the supermarkets on one side of the ocean tell the producers on the other side what their 'exotic' fruits should look like. Moreover, the potential absurdity of this situation manifests itself in the need for tight supervision of the black workforce by the white management. If the fruits are considered by the workforce to be rather ordinary, it would be

Tied in on unequal terms: workers on a fruit farm in Latin America

129

difficult culturally to persuade them, for example, that the pleasantly odd-shaped papaya or the attractively discoloured pitahaya should be rejected on the grounds that it would not appeal to or be recognized by Western consumers. In one sense, this is just another form of unequal cultural exchange.

As distances contract, however, what was once represented as exotic tends increasingly to turn into the familiar. As the social space of producers and consumers contracts, the meanings attributed to the Caribbean fruits may well shift over time, in much the same way that avocado pears 'shed their exotic image to become everyday fruits available, like apples and oranges, throughout the year' (Cook, 1994, p. 244).

To return to the issue of unequal worlds, however, I want to move quickly onto the second example. Rather than worlds separated by long distances, the unequal worlds of the groups we are about to consider share the same place of work, yet live quite different networks of global relations.

Imagine the following scenario (drawn from Allen and Pryke, 1994): the contrived setting is a large, established British merchant bank in the City of London, one which can trace its roots back to the City's inception as a financial centre in the late seventeenth century.

The bank occupies a 'smart' new building; that is, one of the high-technology steel and glass structures which have sprung up in the City of late. Yet the bank still prides itself on practising a traditional culture of finance, especially on the top floors of the building. Here, amidst Victorian wall coverings and recessed bookshelves, the 'gentlemen' dealers conduct their corporate business in the privacy of oak-panelled rooms. Beneath them, some two or three floors below, amidst banks of information technology, screen-based traders deal in 24-hour 'global stock' at a rather more hectic pace.

It is early morning, however, and the trading floors are silent. The building is empty except for the cleaners who have just arrived and the security guards who are nearing the end of their 12-hour shift. The small group of contract cleaners are mostly Colombians who sought work in the UK in the 1970s. The remainder are drawn from a variety of groups – mainly Nigerians and Ghanaians from West Africa. The contract security guards are black English and one is an older, Afro-Caribbean migrant who came to the UK in the 1950s.

The cleaners go about their business, vacuuming the carpets, polishing the floors and dusting down the furnishings. They work as a team, although on separate floors, often divided by choice on the basis of ethnicity. By the time that they have returned the cleaning materials and equipment to the store room in the basement, the first group of financial dealers, all of whom are white English, have entered the building. Silently, they acknowledge the guard at the front entrance and make their way, chattering all the while, up to their desks on one of the trading floors. Before long they are in contact with other traders half way across the world, with one eye on their screens and the other on the animated gestures of their colleagues.

By 9 am the cleaners have left the building and so too have the guards on the night shift. Both groups will have earnt around £3 an hour (at 1994 wage levels) for their efforts.

social distance

At first sight, it may look as if the only global connections involved are the
obvious ones of the financial dealers: the information and communications
networks which connect the world's financial centres. On reflection, however,
there are at least two ways in which the contract cleaners and guards may be
said to be every bit as 'global' in their relationships as the financiers.

The first way is through the cleaning companies and security firms who
employ them. A number of these firms are virtually as multinational in their
business as the merchant banks. Recall the example of ISS, the Danish
cleaning multinational mentioned in section 3.2.1, with its total workforce of
120,000 spread across parts of Europe and the Americas. Moreover, the
largest security firms in the UK today – the likes of Group 4 Securitas, a
Netherlands-based multinational of Swedish parentage, for instance – operate
in dozens of countries worldwide. Both firms are eminently global. A second
set of global relationships arises from the migrant background of much of
the contract workforce of these industries in London. Colombians, Nigerians,
Ghanaians, Afro-Caribbeans, are among those groups who, each in their own
way, have helped to fashion the plurality of cultures evident today in first
world cities like London.

On this account, then, something as straightforward as a merchant bank in a
global city reveals itself as more than the sum of its financial networks. Look
more closely at this one building in the heart of London and it is
increasingly difficult not to see other 'local worlds' made up of cultural and
economic networks which also stretch across the globe. Such worlds, however,
which have been brought into contact with one another through the
globalization of ethnic networks, may still be as remote from one another as
if they were held apart by the barriers of distance. To be a Colombian or a
Nigerian cleaner at a London bank, for instance, may amount to sharing the
same social space as the busy world of international finance, but the
experience is marked by cultural and economic inequalities.

3.3.3   Other worlds

So far, in this section we have spoken solely about the uneven and unequal
nature of global processes and relations. Globalization, in this context, has
been portrayed as the networks of relationships which tie people and places
into the same global space. They share the same social space, whether
brought together over thousands of miles or kilometres or thrown together
in the same streets and cities of the first world. Clearly not everyone is tied

into the global time and space of the rich, industrialized countries, yet one possible implication of all this is that, if you are outside of *their* global geography, you are somehow not part of the global process.

Activity 6 Think about this for a moment. There is clearly a belief here that there is only one global space. On the face of it, this suggests that now, as in the past, 'globalization' is primarily a Western affair. It is the networks of the affluent world, including Japan, which mark out global time. What are we to make of such a 'world view'? Can you think of global networks which cut across or interrupt the time-frame and social space of the West?

One that comes to mind is that of the Islamic world. For many in the West the Muslim world represents a 'political community' which is largely outside of the historical time of the modern West. At worst, the Islamic world is held up as a return to pre-modern times, in terms of economic practices, relationships between men and women, and principles of democratic organization. In this, yet another out-of-scale image, some billion Muslims are portrayed as a kind of transnational political force; a global network centred on the southern and eastern edges of Europe, in North Africa and the Arab-speaking countries, stretching to Pakistan, Bangladesh and Indonesia in the 'Far East' and having a presence 'inside' most Western countries.

Far from being a unified force, however, this kind of imaginative geography distorts our sense of Islamic social space and glosses over the national, ethnic, religious and political differences that make up the Muslim world (see **Beeley, 1995**[*], for an account). In much the same way that a global culture may be said to represent a mix of cultural styles and interpretations, so the Muslim world is made up of particular representations of Islam. The 'fundamentalist' Muslim in Iran, say, or even in London, sees Islam as a global phenomenon differently on a variety of counts from that of a 'Westernized' Muslim in Turkey or from that expressed by a Muslim in the world's largest Islamic state, Indonesia.

Having said that, the Islamic states do share the common experience of having been, at one historical moment or another, part of the colonial time-frame of the West. Directly or indirectly, all the Islamic countries have been tied into the imperial geographies of the West. For some groups and Muslim states, the past experience of this kind of cultural imperialism, coupled with the recent overblown images, held in the West, of a unified Islamic world, have led them to seek among themselves a way of rejecting a Western-led path to globalization. If earlier phases of globalization shaped much of the world in the image of the West, many Islamic societies do not wish to see a repetition of past history. It is in this sense that some Muslims with alternative lifestyles and practices seek to interrupt the global time of the West.

Perhaps you thought of examples other than Islam which represent a kind of 'global alternative' to the Western world? Another possibility is that of the overseas Chinese and the vast social networks which they have constructed across the world. The product of a Chinese diaspora over centuries, their social networks have recently come to the fore in accounts of globalization which acknowledge the increased significance of China in the global economy.

[*] A reference in emboldened type denotes a chapter in another volume of the series.

With 1.1 billion people, China represents another kind of panic in the West, this time economic rather than cultural. The fear, as expressed by many, is that China, along with other Asian economies, is catching up with the developed countries in terms of economic size and that, before long, it may overtake them. History indeed suggests that countries do leap over one another, as, for example, the USA leapt over the UK at the end of the nineteenth century, and a century before that the UK overtook the Dutch. More to the point, today's fast-growing economies have been growing in size more rapidly than ever. On this evidence, then, it is conceivable that China could sweep past today's rich countries and begin to shape the world, if not in its own image, then certainly in the first instance through its worldwide business networks and connections.

Such projections are notoriously hazardous, but what is of interest here is the nature and scale of Chinese social and economic networks. The Asia–Pacific rim in particular, and Asia itself, is cross-cut by family-based business ties and relationships that do not function along formal, Western lines. Since China's 'open door' reforms in 1979, money and investments have been pouring into China through these global networks, drawing attention to the economic power and extent of the Chinese diaspora.

Activity 7 You can gain a sense of how these networks operate by reading the newspaper report by Kieran Cooke which appeared in the *Financial Times* on 14 June 1993 and is reproduced below.

Aside from the geography of the networks, note what Cooke has to say about the social nature of the networks themselves and how they might appear to differ from those in the West.

Emigrant entrepreneurs seize new opportunities back home

By Kieran Cooke in Kuala Lumpur

In September 1893 the imperial authorities in China issued an edict encouraging successful Chinese emigrants to invest in their homeland. The edict proclaimed that the overseas Chinese would in future be welcomed back to China – a reversal of previous policy which had not recognised those who had left China's shores.

Now, 100 years on, China is once again wooing the overseas Chinese to participate in developments at home. And the Chinese diaspora, many of whom are removed from China by several generations, are responding.

While investment in China by US, Japanese and EC interests has been increasing substantially, it is the financial resources of the overseas Chinese which are now beginning to transform many parts of China.

Just how much of China's foreign investment is accounted for by overseas Chinese is hard to gauge. But its influence is plain to see.

Guangdong province in the south has been transformed by capital flowing in from nearby Hong Kong. Businessmen from Taipei are over-running Fujian, the mainland province just across the water from Taiwan. The vast resources of the overseas Shanghainese – some of them the entrepreneurs primarily responsible for the emergence of Hong Kong in the 1950s and 1960s – are now returning home.

Traditionally the overseas Chinese have always been great savers. Taiwan, with 21m people, has foreign exchange reserves of nearly $90bn. Singapore, three quarters of whose 2.8m people are Chinese, has reserves of more than $40bn.

The Chinese dominate the economies of south-east Asian countries. In Indonesia, Thailand, Malaysia and the Philippines it is the Chinese – though often only a small minority – who control trade and run the biggest companies.

Mr Liem Sioe Liong, an Indonesian Chinese, runs the Salim group, believed to be the biggest in the region with an estimated annual turnover of $8bn.

Mr Liem, who left China as a penniless teenager, is now investing millions in China, much of it in property in areas round his birthplace in Fujian province.

Mr Robert Kuok, a Malaysian Chinese, has a business empire mainly involved in commodities and hotels. Mr Kuok is investing in building hotels and commodity processing facilities in various parts of China.

Chinese businesses are traditionally family-run, secretive enterprises. A web of Chinese family concerns stretches throughout east Asia and, increasingly, into China.

For the most part the overseas Chinese avoid China's cumbersome bureaucracy: in many cases they strike informal deals with local groups, often based on family connections.

For some there is a strong emotional attachment to the homeland. But most investments are made for hard-headed commercial reasons. They, like so many others, are intent on making the most of the opportunities available in such a vast market.

Source: *Financial Times*, 14 June 1993, p. 2

Well, to begin with there is the secretive, informal nature of these family-based networks. It is difficult to know exactly what is meant by secretive in this context; however, it may, for example, simply be that the notions of trust involved do not accord with received Western business practice. What is regarded as secretive about a particular culture by those on the 'outside' may be self-evident to those who live by its codes and practices. For the most part, it is the family connections and ethnic ties which drive the networks and, for that very reason, they are likely to be difficult to unravel unless you are part of them.

The informal nature of these connections – *guanxi* – the lifeblood of Chinese businesses, is often rooted in family chains that go back generations. Moreover, such connections may hide the source of the investments flowing back into China from the outside. Much of the money is said to flow *through* the Hong Kong and Taiwanese Chinese communities, although its origins may lie elsewhere in the large Chinese communities in parts of Canada, or in the USA or the UK or, indeed, any one of the South East Asian countries with an active Chinese business community.

Another point of interest raised in the report is the idea that the overseas Chinese demonstrate a strong attachment to their homeland. This, too, is said to represent a layer of *guanxi*: the connections between people with ancestors from the same part of China. Again, it is difficult to know just how much significance to attach to the view that the overseas network has a strong sense of its ancestral roots, although the response to the 'call for investment' from overseas Chinese removed by several generations is itself suggestive of both symbolic and profitable return. Many such returns are indeed linked to the ancestral birthplace or, more broadly, the ethnic region, primarily because that is where the connections are to be found.

The Chinese diaspora and its global network of connections, then, is not, like some parts of the Muslim world, seeking to interrupt the 'time' of the West; rather, its networks cut across Western social space. If those who think that China will before long join the ranks of the world's most dynamic economies are correct, then perhaps the notion of an eastern-led path to globalization will make equal sense.

Summary of section 3.3

o   Global relations, whether economic, cultural or political, are profoundly *uneven* in their geography, locking some people and places into the same social space, whilst by-passing others. Many of the connections and ties which give shape to a 'global world' are centred in the developed North, although changing patterns of movement, mobility and communications are beginning to unravel this geography.

o   Global relations link people across vast tracts of the globe in *unequal* and often vulnerable ways. This has been a characteristic of successive waves of globalization, although as distances recede and the world becomes a 'smaller' place, the unequal nature of global connections may be experienced across the same city or street.

o   Global relations are often portrayed as networks of connections between the West and the rest of the world. In a world that is shrinking in size, an awareness of other global networks, such as those linking Islamic groups or those connecting overseas Chinese to their homeland, holds the potential to disrupt Western-centred views of globalization.

3.4   Conclusion: global imaginations

As both the previous chapters emphasized, to place ourselves in the world, to understand our 'local world' in relation to others, is to exercise our geographical imagination. In this chapter, we have attempted to develop this aspect of our imagination a little further by drawing attention to how globalization draws people into the same *social space* and thus effectively locks them into the same *historical time*. The two aspects are interwoven: if you are drawn into the geographical influence of the developed world, then there is every chance that you will find yourself governed by the dynamic of that world. As we have seen, however, there are many 'global worlds', not all of which are part of the latest wave of Western globalization. And there are 'global worlds' such as those constructed by migrant groups moving to the centres of the developed world which have the capacity to disrupt that time and rhythm.

In one sense, each 'global world' has its own social space – networks of social relationships stretched across the globe. Some of these networks overlap, often on unequal terms, whilst others co-exist in their geographies. What we in the West understand by the 'whole' world is a particular *representation* of its global character: one that, more often than not, is dominated by a network of connections – of ideas, money, communications and so forth – which are centred in the developed world.

Increased talk of the world getting 'smaller' in this context, of a world shrinking in size in the face of revolutions in transport and communications technologies, holds a different meaning for most of the world's population who do not yet have access to a telephone line. Information-rich 'superhighways' are not necessarily part of their geographical imagination. But this is to touch upon the concerns of the next volume in the series, *A Shrinking World?* (Allen and Hamnett, 1995).

References

ALLEN, J. and HAMNETT, C. (eds) (1995) *A Shrinking World? Global Unevenness and Inequality*, Oxford, Oxford University Press in association with The Open University.

ALLEN, J. and PRYKE, M. (1994) 'The production of service space', *Environment and Planning D: Society and Space*, Vol. 12, pp. 453–75.

BEELEY, B. (1995) 'Global options: Islamic alternatives', in Anderson, J., Brook, C. and Cochrane, A. (eds) *A Global World? Reordering Political Space*, Oxford, Oxford University Press in association with The Open Univerisity.

CHAMBERS, I. (1994) *Migrancy, Culture and Identity*, London, Routledge.

COOK, I.J. (1993) 'Constructing the exotic: the case of tropical fruit', paper presented at the annual conference of the Institute of British Geographers, Royal Holloway and Bedford New College, Egham, Surrey, 5–8 January.

COOK, I.J. (1994) 'New fruits and vanity: symbolic production in the global food economy', in Bonanno, A., Busch, L., Friedland, W.H., Gouveia, L. and Mingione, E. (eds) *From Columbus to ConAgra: the Globalization of Agriculture and Food*, Lawrence, KS, University Press of Kansas.

DALBY, S. (1992) 'Ecopolitical discourse: "environmental security" and political geography', *Progress in Human Geography*, Vol. 16, No. 4, pp. 503–22.

DICKEN, P. (1992) *Global Shift: the Internationalization of Economic Activity*, (2nd edn), London, Paul Chapman.

DONAGHU, M.T. and BARFF, R. (1990) 'Nike just did it: international subcontracting and flexibility in athletic footwear production', *Regional Studies*, Vol. 24, No. 6, pp. 537–52.

HANNERZ, U. (1992) *Cultural Complexity: Studies in the Social Organization of Meaning*, New York, Columbia University Press.

HELD, D. (1991) 'Democracy, the nation state and the global system', in Held, D. (ed.) *Political Theory Today*, Cambridge, Polity Press.

OHMAE, K. (1990) *The Borderless World: Power and Strategy in the Interlinked Economy*, London, Fontana.

OHMAE, K. (1993) 'The rise of the region state', *Foreign Affairs*, Spring, pp. 78–87.

ROBINS, K. (1991) 'Tradition and translation: national culture in its global context', in Corner, J. and Harvey, S. (eds) *Enterprise and Heritage: Crosscurrents of National Culture*, London, Routledge.

SAID, E.W. (1994) *Culture and Imperialism*, London, Vintage.

UNITED NATIONS (1993) *World Investment Report 1993: Transnational Corporations and Integrated International Production*, United Nations Conference on Trade and Development, Programme on Transnational Corporations, New York, United Nations.

WORLD BANK (1994) *Adjustment in Africa: Reforms, Results and the Road Ahead*, Washington, DC, World Bank.

Reading A: Ian J. Cook, 'Constructing the exotic: the case of tropical fruit' _____

[...]

1   The chain

[...]

Let me try to describe this system, then: the fruit is grown year round on three small farms in Jamaica and sold fresh by all the major British supermarket chains. From seed to shelf, this involves the massive day-to-day co-ordination of people and things. Each fruit's journey begins with the seeds taken from the fruit of admired trees, which are planted, and continually watered, fertilized, pruned and sprayed with pesticides as they grow. After a period of three or four months, these trees enter a cycle of budding, flowering and fruiting which *can* provide an uninterrupted supply of export-quality fruit for up to two years. The fruits are left to grow until they verge on ripeness or 'turn', when they are picked, put into crates on a picking trailer, driven to the packing house. There, they are washed in a fungicide solution, weighed and passed on to be wrapped and boxed, or rejected, depending on their size, shape and level of scarring. When full, these boxes are stacked in the back of the packing house and, later, loaded onto a truck which is driven to the airport in Kingston. Here, they are unloaded, checked through customs, sniffed for drugs by specially trained dogs, and then loaded into containers which are placed in the hold of a scheduled passenger jet *en route* to London.

On their arrival at Gatwick, they are passed through customs again, transferred from their containers onto another truck and driven to their prepacker's depot. Here, they are unloaded, checked against the supermarkets' specifications, regraded and rejected if necessary, and usually individually stickered with the supermarkets' 'own brand' labels which contain a barcode and advice on their preparation and eating. After this, they are reboxed, ripened if necessary, stacked with boxes full of other fruits and vegetables for dispatch, and loaded onto yet another truck. From here, they are driven to the supermarkets' regional warehouses, where they are unloaded, checked again, loaded onto numerous other trucks with other commodities and driven to the individual stores. Once there, they are unloaded, checked, displayed for sale, removed from the shelf either to be placed in a shopper's trolley, scanned through the checkout and taken home or, after their sell-by dates are passed, to be thrown into the fruit department's reject bins and discarded.

And the chain from farm to supermarket and beyond by no means connects only the people involved in *these* practices. I could also include those who have produced the inputs and services drawn on within it. All of these have their own commodity systems stretching between different sites of production and consumption and, therefore, we can say that, despite appearances, an incalculable number of people all over the place are essential to the continuing arrival of this one fruit on the supermarket shelf in the UK.

2 The stories

I have pieced together this commodity system from stories told to me by a number of people working within it, as well as from newspapers, trade journals and other archival sources. The majority of these came from the perspectives either of the farm's black workforce and white management or the supermarkets' exotic fruit buyers.[1] Among other things, I asked them all, mostly on tape, what their work entailed, how they had ended up doing it, and what they thought about it. And, very basically, these stories go as follows: the farm was set up by a young white couple in the late 1980s, he Jamaican and she English. His English grandparents had moved to the island with their families, around the time of the Second World War, to work as engineers in two of its sugar factories. Born and brought up there until the age of eight, he was sent away to public school in the UK where, because of his accent, he was initially subject to the type of racist abuse usually suffered by Afro-Caribbean people. Spending Christmases and summers with his family in Jamaica, he eventually wound up at agricultural college back in Britain, where he met his future wife, the sister of a college mate. When she was in her late teens she, her brother and sister had each inherited several hundred thousand pounds.

In the early 1980s, they married and moved to live in Jamaica, where they eventually found work on a sugar estate, he as a plant engineer and she as a clerical worker. A few years later, he was offered work elsewhere on the island on a farm owned by a fabulously wealthy American family as a tax write-off come tropical retreat. There, he ended up working on a pioneering project to grow the fruit commercially. The owners invested approximately one million US dollars in the first crop which failed but, with the management team having learned by their mistakes, the second crop was successful and the farm began to make money from it. And much of

this was thanks to the Israeli expatriate manager who had come to Jamaica to work on a large strawberry project which had failed. Using his connections, he had been able to set up links with an Israeli importer in the UK who supplied fresh fruit to the major British supermarket chains.

The couple soon left, though, because of disagreements with the owner over pay and conditions. Drawing on his experience as the first graduate of this fruit 'school', they managed to raise several million Jamaican dollars from a development bank which raised capital from selling excess American milk powder, dumped as 'aid', on the Jamaican market. He, ironically, had had to put up his parents' dairy farm as collateral. They then rented some land surrounding the ruins of a former sugar estate which, under new ownership in the early 1960s, was entirely switched over to the grazing of cattle. Out of these ruins, they built an English country cottage with a flower garden and badminton court paid for, like most of their material possessions, out of her inheritance.

Within the first six months or so, they were employing around 90 black people from the surrounding areas, initially to set up the fields and buildings and eventually to tend, pick, sort, pack and ship the fruit. Many of them had been either unemployed or working as casual labourers on building sites along the coast. In addition, key workers had been brought in from the other farm. All were given the opportunity for regular work with medical insurance, subsidized lunches and, although not unionized, roughly equal pay to the surrounding unionized sugar workers who did not enjoy such benefits. Contact with the Israeli importers in the UK was maintained as were others developed with firms in the United States in a tactical move designed to prevent the dependence on just one overseas market.

Meanwhile, largely as a result of economic liberalization and structural adjustment programmes imposed on the Jamaican Government by the World Bank (which, incidentally, led George Bush to praise Jamaica as the jewel in the developing free market Caribbean), exporters were allowed to hold their earnings in foreign exchange accounts rather than suffering either long delays as the Central Bank converted their Jamaican dollars or taking short cuts through the black market. Over the same period, the Jamaican dollar became massively devalued, making their fruit more competitive on the world stage through effectively slashing both the value of their loan and their workers' wages. These wages have increased over this time, but by no means at the same pace as inflation which, generated in an economy which has traditionally produced what it has not consumed and consumed what it has not produced (Beckford, 1985), is highly dependent on fluctuations in the exchange rate, particularly between the Jamaican dollar and the pound and US dollar.

In this context, the manager, his wife and their white friends would often frown on what they saw as the laziness, ignorance, wastefulness, sexual overactivity, lying and childishness in many of their workers. Historically, these stereotypical characteristics can be seen as white colonial 'inventions' which, throughout the development of 'cultures of colonization' in plantation societies, were treated as 'discoveries' and often violently acted upon (Hulme, 1986; Taussig, 1987). And, in the immediate context of this farm's 'culture', these were regularly reinforced when the packing house supervisor accompanied his boss on long car journeys across the island. Here, the latter would grill the former for the 'juicy gossip' about what the workers had been 'up to', which, itself, was unreliably generated out of the combination of jokes and maliciously made up 'bad stories' which continually went around the packing house. Yet, the manager seemed to take these 'inventions' as true, saying to me on one occasion something like: 'If only they knew what I know they've been up to. But I don't let on'. While he and his wife often expressed a great affection for their employees, what they saw as 'their attitude' to work was treated as a serious obstacle to the prosperity of them all because the farm had to run to tight schedules and specifications to make any money in the export market. So, he made sure that they were always under a heavy supervisory gaze, particularly in the packing house, and, using his command of patois, he gave his instructions through a combination of seriousness and joking, threats and promises, bluffs and counterbluffs, which he referred to as 'sweeting them up'.

For their part, many of the women who worked in the packing house (where I spent much of my time) complained about the supervisory eyes which were constantly on them. They complained about the 'bad stories' that were told about them by their co-workers which resulted in few of them discussing openly their feelings about pay and conditions, believing that anyone but their closest friends would rat on them to the management. As a consequence of this, they spent most of their time 'running jokes' with each other to pass the time. They also complained that taxes were drawn from their wages which, although allowing the farm to get an export license from the government, did not appear to provide them with much in the way of civic amenities.

Overall, most agreed that the job was nothing special and just about paid their bills, although this was becoming less and less the case as the prices of basic commodities such as rice, chicken and light bills continued to rise dramatically. Working with these fruits, mundane to them but exotic to their eventual consumers, was not going to improve their lives drastically. With just less than a day's pay, the vast majority of them could afford to buy just one of them in a British supermarket if they ever got to travel there. At best, the money they earned allowed them to buy a few little things they might not have had otherwise. And, despite his increasing wealth and their deepening poverty, they appeared to believe that they had a relatively good boss.

From here, I want to move on to talk about JAMPRO – the Jamaican Government's export development agency. Seeing the apparent success of the first farm's experiment with this fruit, they set up a programme to 'facilitate' further farming enterprises of this type.

Their aim was to keep those people in charge of projects already up and running in contact with both potential future investors and overseas markets. Here, the fact that these two farms were *seen* to be successful was important on three counts. First, for visiting trade delegations: JAMPRO officials took such delegations who would potentially invest in export-oriented production on tours of one or other of these farms because they were highly mechanized, efficient and almost 'Western' and would, they hoped, counter any images of backward farming practices that these people may have had about Jamaica. Second, for potential growers/investors: by the look of them, these farms gave the impression that there was heaps of money in growing this fruit, despite the fact that I had been told that this wealth was, on the one hand, that of an American multi-millionaire, and, on the other, the result of an inheritance. But, as the couple running the latter farm told me, 'Try telling them your brand new Mitsubishi Shogun wasn't bought with money made from this fruit. They just won't believe you.'[2] Finally, for Jamaica at large: here, three documentaries had been made for national television about these farms, stressing their successes and, from watching them, the farm managers can be seen as the 'great white hopes' of Jamaican export agriculture, particularly with sugar going slowly down the drain.

On the other side of the Atlantic, both before and after my stint in Jamaica, I spoke with some exotic fruit buyers working for three of the major British supermarket chains, becoming convinced early on that it was they (along with their marketing colleagues and technologists) who were largely responsible for articulating the sourcing and consumption practices of this and other exotic fruits. Grouped around different types of fresh produce, their job was to fashion a range of produce, prices and quality standards not only out of what they thought their customers would buy, but also what their suppliers could provide and what levels of turnover and profit their bosses demanded.

Their work seemed to revolve around notions of 'quality' and 'value for money' of the produce within their remits. These were constantly under negotiation with a range of trustworthy suppliers and were set out as a series of *specifications* – measures of each item's price, seasonal sourcing details, quality (size, weight per case, internal pressure and sugar content), as well as more 'subjective' accounts of their 'perfect', 'acceptable' and 'unacceptable' forms by shape, blemish level, colour and the level of ripeness they would appear with on the shelf. One buyer told me that 2 per cent of each shipment arriving at their distribution depots was tested against these specifications and, if unacceptable, the entire shipment could be returned to the supplier without payment.

On another level, the importance of a strict adherence to 'quality' standards seemed to stretch well beyond the buyers' offices and the produce aisles they had to fill. In the late 1980s, fresh fruit and vegetables had gained a strong presence in the supermarkets' annual reports. These appear, then, as part of a corporate identity so, as a senior manager told me:

I think the papaya, pitahaya, babacos, lollos, lulos, foyoyas – all these things – ... are a statement about [us]. ... 'Good food costs less at XXXXXX' and XXXXXX has a statement of 'The right product at the right price' – that's the marketing mix.

It seemed that buying teams were not only responsible for choosing a range of produce, setting its specifications and, perhaps, improving the image of their company, though: it was also their job to seek consent for these choices in the lives of people placed all along the commodity systems involved. Reaching out to the consumer, for instance, within the confines of their budgets, they wrote and commissioned artwork for the leaflets and labels often found alongside and attached to their produce. With exotic fruits, these were seen as essential for their successful introduction to the market because, and I was told:

One of the problems with exotic fruit is that they're a bit like armadillos – you can't get into the damn things! You've got to have an instruction manual on how to eat it and what to do with it.

So, you are presented with a number of suggestions for their preparation (for example, how to slice up a mango into cubes) and a couple of reasonably familiar recipes to place this new thing into.

The buyers also had to keep track of what was 'going on' in the market-place and, in doing so, they appeared to rely on a somewhat haphazard combination of ideas gleaned from market research, four or five exotic fruit books, articles in trade journals, letters from customers, media coverage, what their rivals were selling at what price, and the daily rounds of meetings, telephone calls and faxes with, to and from their store managers, colleagues, bosses and suppliers.

What is perhaps most interesting in all this, though, is that, in the context of their isolation from much of the processes and people bringing these fruits to them, they also made the occasional visit to inspect farms in the tropics – part of the supermarkets' claim to 'care' about what went on 'down the line'. Here, amid their inspections of the fields and facilities to judge whether they would produce a predictable stream of good fruit costing less, all told me they had been shocked by, or had heard shocking stories about, the obvious poverty of the people who made much of this possible. Getting back to the office, though, they had to throw these concerns out of the window and get on with their jobs.

3 The understanding

[…] I would like to confess that I often doubted whether these stories were told to me as they might be to anybody else, or whether I had understood them as anybody else would.

[…]

By stressing the social nature of my encounters with these […] peoples […], I cannot claim to be merely extracting parts of an overall story and, perhaps, neither can anyone else. As researchers, I believe that the stories 'we' tell about 'other' peoples and places, as well as the stories 'we' tell about 'ourselves' and the places where 'we' live and work (whoever 'we' think 'we' and 'they' are) have to be seen in the light of the performance of

culture. Here, parallels can be drawn between Michael Taussig's discussion of the history of encounters between colonized and colonizers in Latin America where 'assumed meanings met with assumed meanings to form strange codependencies and culture itself – (a) culture of colonization [which] … bound Indian understandings of white understandings of Indians to white understandings of Indian understandings of whites' (Taussig, 1987, p. 109). Taking this kind of perspective, it seems bizarre to me that, in doing social, cultural, economic, whatever, research, it should be okay to ignore that research is *itself* a product of social, cultural, economic, whatever, relations, whether it be ethnographic or mediated by other people's texts and numbers.

Thus it is necessary to get away from a position in which 'we' in the centre have traditionally treated 'places' and 'peoples' as things to draw lines *around* and towards one where we draw lines *between* them (Massey, 1991). In the field of gastropolitics, 'they' are inside 'us'. Our supermarkets are stocked with a great variety of foods produced all over the globe which, if bought, prepared and eaten, provide 'us' with raw materials through which 'we' can reproduce 'our' selves both *physically* – through ingesting their fat, mineral, carbohydrate, vitamin, roughage and water contents – as well as *socially* – through demonstrating 'our' cultural capital of knowing how to select, prepare and eat these foods 'properly'. So, through 'our' everyday food-consumption practices, 'we' become involved in a complex and connected 'post-colonial gastropolitics' and take an active part in the plays of domination and resistance which delimit the possibilities for 'third world development'.

Notes

1 In this case, the adjectives 'black' and 'white' are taken from classifications of 'race' commonly used both in the British binary and in the more complex Jamaican pigmentocracy (see James, 1992).
2 This quotation has been somewhat fabricated to get the point over while not explicitly identifying them by their fruit or car.

References

BECKFORD, G. (1985) 'Caribbean peasantry in the confines of the plantation mode of production', *International Social Science Journal*, Vol. 37, No. 3, pp. 410–14.

HULME, P. (1986) *Colonial Encounters: Europe and the Native Caribbean 1492–1797*, London, Routledge.

JAMES, W. (1992) 'Migration, racism and identity: the Caribbean experience in Britain', *New Left Review*, No. 193, pp. 15–55.

MASSEY, D. (1991) 'A global sense of space', *Marxism Today*, June, pp. 24–9.

TAUSSIG, M. (1987) *Shamanism, Colonialism and the Wild Man: a Study in Terror and Healing*, Chicago, IL, University of Chicago Press.

Source: Cook, 1993, pp. 3–19

Acknowledgements

We have made every attempt to obtain permission to reproduce material in this book. Copyright holders of material which has not been acknowledged should contact the Rights Department at The Open University.

Grateful acknowledgement is made to the following sources for permission to reproduce material in this volume:

Text

Chapter 1: Schwimmer, E. (1992) 'Land use map presented in congress seeks to affirm Indian rights in the Mosquitia' and 'Miskito musician gives congress "upbeat note"', *Honduras This Week*, Vol. 5, No. 37, 26 September 1992; Zoba, W.M. (1992) '500 years later, indian groups claim their place on map', *Honduras This Week*, Vol. 5, No. 37, 26 September 1992; extracts from *Focus On Images*, The Save The Children Fund; William Wordsworth, *Lyrical Ballads*, 1798, extract from 'Tintern Abbey': The Wordsworth Trust; *Reading A:* Wright, D.R. (1993) 'Maps with a message', *Geographical Magazine*, January 1993; *Reading B:* extracts from *The Old Patagonian Express* by Paul Theroux, pp. 61–3, 77, 79, 81–2, Hamish Hamilton 1979, copyright © Cape Cod Scriveners Co., 1979. Reproduced by permission of Hamish Hamilton Ltd. Also by permission of Aitken, Stone & Wylie Ltd; *Chapter 2:* Ward, D. (1994) 'Liverpool, city with an image problem, seeks slick slogan', *The Guardian*, 21 May 1994; *Reading A:* Grant, L. (1987) *Women Workers and the Sexual Division of Labour: Liverpool 1890–1939*, PhD Thesis, University of Liverpool; *Reading B:* McManus, K. (1994) *Céilís, Jigs and Ballads: Irish Music in Liverpool*, Institute of Popular Music; *Reading C:* McManus, K. (1994) *'Nashville of the North': Country Music in Liverpool*, Institute of Popular Music; *Chapter 3:* Bremner, C. (1993) 'Mitterrand enlists old empire in linguistic defence of Gaul', *The Times*, 19 October 1993, © Times Newspapers Ltd. 1993; Cooke, K. (1993) 'Emigrant entrepreneurs seize new opportunities back home', *Financial Times*, 14 June 1993; *Reading A:* Cook, I. (1993) 'Constructing the exotic: the case of tropical fruit', paper presented at the Institute of British Geographers' Annual Conference, Royal Holloway and Bedford New College, Egham, Surrey, 5–8 January 1993, © Ian J. Cook.

Figures

Figure 1.1: base map provided by MundoCart/CD – a digital product of the Petroconsultants Group. Copyrights apply; *Figures A2, A10: Pocket Atlas* by Jill and David Wright published by Kingfisher Books. Copyright © Grisewood and Dempsey 1983; *Figures A3, A6, A7, A8, A9, A11, A12, A13, A14, A15, A17:* courtesy of David Wright; *Figure 2.2:* Duignan, P. and Gann, L. (1985) *The United States and Africa: A History*, Cambridge University Press; *Figure 2.5:* Wolf, E. (1982) *Europe and the People Without History*, University of California Press. Reproduced by permission; *Figure 3.2:* UNCTAD (1993) *World Investment Report 1993, Transnational Corporations and Integrated International Production*, copyright © United Nations 1993, All rights reserved; *Figure 3.3:* Held, D. (1991) *Political Theory Today*, Basil Blackwell Ltd.

Map

p. 8: Indigenous lands of the Honduran Mosquitia – 1992: zones of subsistence. A map made for and presented at the First Congress on Indigenous Lands of the Mosquitia, 22–23 September 1992, in Tegucigalpa, Honduras. A project administered by Mosquitia Pawisa (MOPAWI) and Mosquitia Asla Takanka (MASTA). Project design and management by Peter H. Herlihy PhD, Southeastern Louisiana University and Andrew P. Leake MA, MOPAWI. Information on land use compiled through the administration of questionnaires in community meetings by native Indian surveyors: Moisés Alemán, Paulino Bossen, Daniel Castellón, Quintín Castro, Máximo Chow, Dionisio Cruz, Simón Greham P., Duval Haylock, Daniel Kiath, Olegario López, Gilberto Maibeth, Hernán Martínez, Manuel Martínez, Eduardo Padilla, Electerio Pineda K., Ricardo Ramírez, Javier Rimundo G., Tomás Rivas, Cecilio Tatallón, Elmer Waldemar, Sinito Waylan and Edimor Wood M. Project sponsored by Cultural Survival, Inc., with the collaboration of Comisión Nacional del Medio Ambiente y Desarrollo (CONAMA), Federación Indígena Tawahka de Honduras (FITH), Inter American Foundation (IAF), Interamerican Geodetic Survey (IAGS), Instituto Geográfico Nacional (IGN), Caribbean Conservation Corporation, Pew Charitable Trusts, Wildlife Conservation International and Instituto Hondureño de Antropología e Historia (IHAH). Technical field assistants: José Ramiro Andino (IGN), Prof. Cirilo Felman (MASTA), Nathan Pravia Lacayo (MOPAWI), Lic. Adalberto Padilla (MOPAWI), Héctor Ramírez (IGN) and Lic. Aurelio Ramos (MOPAWI).

Photographs/cartoons

p. 6: Eric Schwimmer/*Honduras This Week*; *p. 12:* Suyapa Carias/*Honduras This Week*; *p. 25:* The Save The Children Fund/photographs by J. Hammond, Neil Cooper and Peter Charlesworth; *p. 35:* Bob Haverluck/Leeds Postcards; *p. 36:* Oxfam (Belfast)/Collection Dibujos, Barcelona; *p. 63:* Mary Evans Picture Library; *p. 68:* J. Allan Cash; *p. 81:* Peter Kaye/copyright Apple Corps Ltd; *p. 99:* courtesy of Kevin McManus of the Institute of Popular Music, University of Liverpool, and of Sean McNamara. Photograph by Eric Durkin; *p. 101:* copyright Kevin McManus; *p. 104:* courtesy of the Institute of Popular Music, University of Liverpool, and of Bunter Perkins/copyright Butlins; *p. 118:* Barbara Smith; *p. 120:* John Maier/Still Pictures; *p. 125:* Mark Edwards/Still Pictures; *p. 129:* Carlos Reyes-Manzo/Andes Press Agency.

Colour plate section

Plate 1: copyright the British Museum; *Plate 2:* The William L. Clements Library, The University of Michigan; *Plate 3:* from the American Geographical Society Collection, University of Wisconsin-Milwaukee Library; *Plate 4:* courtesy of the Board of Trustees of the National Museums and Galleries on Merseyside; *Plate 5:* The Royal Geographical Society; *Plate 6:* Mary Evans Picture Library; *Plate 7:* Standard Chartered Bank/DMB & B Financial; *Plate 8:* Tom Van Sant/The GeoSphere Project, Santa Monica/Science Photo Library.

Index